The Ilkhanid Heartland:
Hasanlu Tepe (Iran) Period I

Frontispiece. Reconstructed design from a Lājvardīnah jar (HAS 62-10).

University Museum Monograph 120

THE ILKHANID HEARTLAND: HASANLU TEPE (IRAN) PERIOD I

Michael D. Danti

Hasanlu Excavation Reports

Robert H. Dyson, Jr., General Editor

Volume II

University of Pennsylvania Museum of Archaeology and Anthropology
Philadelphia

Copyright © 2004
By the University of Pennsylvania Museum of Archaeology and Anthropology
3260 South Street
Philadelphia, PA 19104

First Edition

All rights reserved

CIP data available at the Library of Congress

ISBN 1-931707-66-9

MICHAEL D. DANTI is a research specialist for the Hasanlu Publications Project of the Near Eastern Section of the University of Pennsylvania Museum. He also serves as the field director of the Museum's excavations at Tell es-Sweyhat, Syria. He received his Ph.D. from the University of Pennsylvania in Anthropology in 2000.

Printed in the United States of America on acid-free paper

To

Caroline G. Dosker, camp manager and registrar of the Hasanlu excavations (1957-62), and to the representatives of the Iranian Archaeological Service to Hasanlu between 1956 and 1962: Taghi Assefi (1956-59), Ali Akbar Asgharian (1958, 1959), S. Gandjavi (1960), Mahmoud Kordovani (1960), Reza Mustafi (1960), and Shahrukh Mushapour (1962).

PUBLISHED WITH THE ASSISTANCE OF THE KEVORKIAN FOUNDATION

Contents

List of Illustrations xi
Foreword, *Robert H. Dyson, Jr.* xiii
Acknowledgments xv
Abbreviations xvii
1. Hasanlu Tepe and the Surrounding Area 1
2. History of the Excavation of Period I, 1956–62 7
3. The Southern High Mound 11
    Building I 11
    Building II 14
    Period I Ceramics: General Characteristics 22
    Period I Ceramics from Building I and Surrounding Area 23
4. The Northwest High Mound 27
    Building III 27
    Building IV 31
    The Fortification Wall 33
    Period I Ceramics from Building III and Surrounding Area 33
    Period I Ceramics from Building IV and Surrounding Area 36
5. The Northern Stratigraphic Trench 43
6. The Northeast High Mound 49
    Building V 49
    Period I Ceramics from Building V and the Surrounding Area 49
7. Regional Reconnaissance, Surveys, and Excavations 59
8. Summary and Conclusions 63
Bibliography 69
Plates 75
Index 93

Illustrations

Color Plates, following p. 46

A   Hasanlu I: Glazed ceramics from Buildings I and III.
B   Hasanlu I: Glazed ceramics from Building III and surrounding area.
C   Hasanlu I: Glazed ceramics from Building III and surrounding area.
D   Hasanlu I: Glazed ceramics from Building IV and surrounding area.
E   Hasanlu I: Glazed ceramics from Building IV and surrounding area.
F   Hasanlu I: Glazed ceramics from various contexts at Hasanlu Tepe.
G   Takht-i Sulaimān: Glazed and incised ware.
H   Takht-i Sulaimān and Dinkha Tepe: Various glazed wares.

Figures

1	The Near East showing the location of Hasanlu Tepe and other Ilkhanid sites	xviii
2	The Ushnu-Sūldūz valley showing the location of Hasanlu Tepe and other sites of the Saljūq and Ilkhanid periods	3
3	Hasanlu Tepe: 1936 sketch map by Sir Aurel Stein	4
4	Hasanlu Tepe: Topographic plan of the High Mound	5
5	Hasanlu I: Plan of Buildings I and II, southern High Mound	12
6	Key to sections	13
7	Hasanlu I: East section of Building I, Rooms 1, 2, and 5	15
8	Hasanlu I: East-west section through oven and flue segments in Building I, Room 4	16
9	Hasanlu I: South section of Building I, Rooms 1 and 4	17
10	Hasanlu I: East section of Building I, Room 8	18
11	Hasanlu I: North section of Building I, Rooms 1 and 7	19
12	Hasanlu I: Small finds and ceramics from Building I	21
13	Hasanlu I: Plan of Building III, northwestern High Mound	24
14	Hasanlu I: Small finds from Building III and surrounding area	29
15	Hasanlu I: Plan of Building IV, the northern High Mound	32
16	Hasanlu I: Small finds from Building IV and surrounding area	35
17	Hasanlu I: North section of Building IV	37
18	Hasanlu I: Ceramics from Building III and surrounding area	39
19	Hasanlu I: Ceramics from Building IV and surrounding area	41
20	Hasanlu I: Operations I, VII L-M, and VII J-K, the northern High Mound	44
21	Hasanlu I: West section of Operation VII J-K	46
22	Hasanlu I: West section of Operation VII L-M	47
23	Hasanlu I: Plan of Building V, northeastern High Mound	48
24	Hasanlu I: Small finds from Building V and surrounding area	51
25	Hasanlu I: Red ware ceramics from Building V and surrounding area	53
26	Hasanlu I: Ceramics from Building V and surrounding area	55

27　Hasanlu I: Ceramics from various contexts 57
28　Takht-i Sulaimān: Red ware ceramics from the 1956 Reconnaissance 60
29　Hasanlu I: Site reconstruction based on aerial photos, Stein's 1936 sketch map, and the
　　1956–62 excavations 65

Plates 75

A　Aerial view of Hasanlu Tepe and the villages of Hasanlu and Aminlu taken in 1937 by Erich Schmidt.
B　Aerial view of Hasanlu Tepe and the village of Hasanlu taken from the southeast in 1957 by Harold Josef.
C　Aerial view of Hasanlu Tepe in 1962 taken by Vaughn Crawford from the south looking north.
D　Operation XXXIX (Grid BB28) Building I Rooms 1 and 4.
E　Operation XXXIX (Grid BB28) from the west.
F　Operation XXXIX (Grid BB28) from the southwest.
G　Operation XXXIV (CC30) taken in 1960 from the northeast.
H　Plaster with wood lathe impressions from Building III Room 2.
J　Grid U23 Building III Room 3.
K　Objects from Building III.
L　Grid U23 Building III Room 4 looking east.
M　Grid U23 Building III Room 4 looking west.
N　Grid T23 Building III Room 6 looking north.
O　Grid T23 Building III Room 6 looking southwest.
P　Lājvardīnah ware jar sherds.
Q　Objects from Operation L and other contexts.
R　Buff ware lantern from Operation L.

Foreword

The site of Hasanlu Tepe, Iran, is mainly known for its important archaeological sequence from the earlier periods of the Iron Age.

On the morning of September 8, 1936, the British archaeologist Sir Aurel Stein arrived at the site of Hasanlu, south of Lake Urmīyeh east of the road to Naqadeh. Stein was near the end of his long, productive survey trip through western Iran, the last stage of which led him across the Ushnu-Sūldūz Valley along the border between the Kurdistān and Āzarbaijān provinces of Iran (Figures 1 and 2; Stein 1940). Stein recognized the site's importance and carried out small-scale excavations, the first scientific work there.

Hasanlu, the largest site in Sūldūz, lies in a depression separated from Lake Urmīyeh to the north by a small hill chain and the Gadār River to the south by a ridge. The site itself stands approximately 25 m above the adjacent plain. The central high or citadel mound is about 200 m across, with steep north and south slopes. The western slope is slightly less steep, while the eastern slope descends much more gradually.

On July 25, 1937, at 8 A.M., Erich F. Schmidt flew over Hasanlu as part of his aerial survey of Iran (Schmidt 1940); the photographs then taken (nos. AE 650 and 651), however, were never published. In 1960 Dr. Schmidt kindly provided us with prints of these pictures and permission to publish them (Plate A). They provide excellent documentation for the setting of the site but add little to our knowledge of the High Mound but that a military trench already existed.

When Jason Paige, Taghi Assefi, and I arrived at the site in 1956 the military trench was very visible. The surface of the mound was covered with dense grass except for a wide strip, which followed around the wall line, about a meter wide, with no evidence of grass or brickwork. We thought that the wall had perhaps been built of packed mud that had melted away leaving a bare discolored grayish zone. This pattern is visible in the air photograph taken in 1957 (Plate B) by Harold Joseph, the American consul in Tabrīz, and in Vaughn Crawford's air view of 1962 (Plate C). Visible in the Joseph photograph is the outer military trench with gun emplacements and the inner circumvallation making almost a right angle at its northeastern corner. Our 1956-57 north-south exploratory trench (Operations I, II, and VII) appears at the top center of the High Mound with the central depression at its end (to the left). The raking light shows that some relief still existed along the line of the inner circumvallation, although this was virtually invisible at ground level. It was possible, we thought, that there had been a stone foundation, but our excavations in 1956 and later produced no such evidence. Nor was there any cultural debris indicating an Islamic occupation other than rare sherds. This was not surprising since, as a rule, grass-covered mounds like this do not yield much in the way of surface material unless badly disturbed. Thus, while indirect evidence suggested the presence of some kind of Islamic occupation, there was really little of substance to go on. The Islamic level at the top (Period I) was ephemeral in most places.

After painstaking review of the field records from Hasanlu for the period 1956–62, Michael Danti has been able to integrate and interpret the scattered excavation data to produce this important volume documenting the little-excavated Ilkhanid period of the late 13th to early 14th centuries A.D. Given the rarity of such documented material we are delighted with the result. The almost complete lack of excavations at small rural settlements from this period make it extremely difficult for researchers to move beyond historical records in studies of the mixed economy practiced at this time, integrating newly introduced patterns of nomadic pastoralism with farming. This report represents one small, but critical step in what we hope will be a new direction in the archaeology of northwestern Iran.

Robert H. Dyson, Jr.
Project Director

ACKNOWLEDGMENTS

I would like first and foremost to thank Robert H. Dyson, Jr., for allowing me to undertake this project, generously providing access to the Hasanlu archives, and taking time out of his schedule to discuss the Hasanlu excavations for countless hours. Without his continued encouragement, guidance, and intellectual input this volume would not exist.

Funds for the 1956–62 Hasanlu excavations were generously provided by Dr. George C. Browning, Mr. and Mrs. Rudolphe de Schauensee, Dr. Robert H. Dyson, Jr., Mrs. Robert M. Green, Mrs. Nancy Grace, Ms. Mary Virginia Harris, Prof. J. R. Kantor, Mrs. Penny von Kersburg, Mrs. Michael J. Kocialek, Dr. and Mrs. Austin Lamont, Mr. Howard Levy, Mr. Lionel Levy, Dr. Edith Porada, Mr. Peter Paanaker, Commodore John K. Richards, Mr. Basil Saffer, Dr. Preston Smith, Dr. A. D. Tushingham, and Professor T. Cuyler Young, Sr. Institutional donors included the Archaeological Service of Iran, the Explorer's Club of New York, General Shale Products Corporation, the Kevorkian Foundation, the Metropolitan Museum of Art, the National Science Foundation, the University of Pennsylvania Museum, and the Walter E. Hering Fund of the University of Pennsylvania Museum.

I want to single out for thanks the staff who served on the Hasanlu excavations between 1956 and 1962, when Period I occupation was uncovered, for special recognition. The superlative work of the late Vaughn Crawford especially comes to mind. Through this project, I have developed a deep respect for the generations of Hasanlu staff who came before me.

I owe an equal debt of gratitude to the members of the Archaeological Service of Iran who facilitated the Hasanlu excavations, both in the Iran Bastan Museum (now the National Museum of Iran) and in the field.

At the University of Pennsylvania, my thanks go to the Board of Overseers and to Jeremy A. Sabloff, Williams Director of the University of Pennsylvania Museum, for their continued support of the Hasanlu Publications Project. Richard L. Zettler, Associate Curator-in-Charge of the Near Eastern Section, has played a central role in seeing me through the process of completing this research. Shannon White, the Fowler/Van Santvoord Keeper, facilitated my work from the beginning, providing access to the collections, research support, and the critical eye of a fellow archaeologist. Maude de Schauensee, Editor of the Hasanlu Project, was involved in the production of this volume from the time much of the material was excavated, processed, and housed at the Museum, to its final publication. Her dedication to the Hasanlu Project inspires us all. Without the herculean labors of Mary Virginia Harris, Registrar of the Hasanlu Publication Archives, the Hasanlu excavation records would not be the valuable, user-friendly research tool they are today. Her presence is palpable in all we do.

I owe the illustrators of the Hasanlu Project with whom I have worked—Denise Hoffman, Jana Fisher, Laura Flaxman, Ted Hemmaplardh, and Kimberly Leaman—a great deal for their impeccable work and patience. I want to recognize and thank Katy Blanchard, William "Brad" Hafford, and Kevin L. Danti for providing often-needed morale-building support.

Finally, I must express my abiding love for my wife Samantha and our children, Nathaniel and Kersten. They have ungrudgingly sacrificed so much over the years as I pursue my dream of practicing archaeology.

Abbreviations

d.	diameter
HAS	Hasanlu Field Number
l.	length
MET	Metropolitan Museum of Art, New York
Rm.	room
Str.	stratum
Surf.	surface
th.	thickness
TM	Tehran Museum
UPM	University of Pennsylvania Museum
w.	width

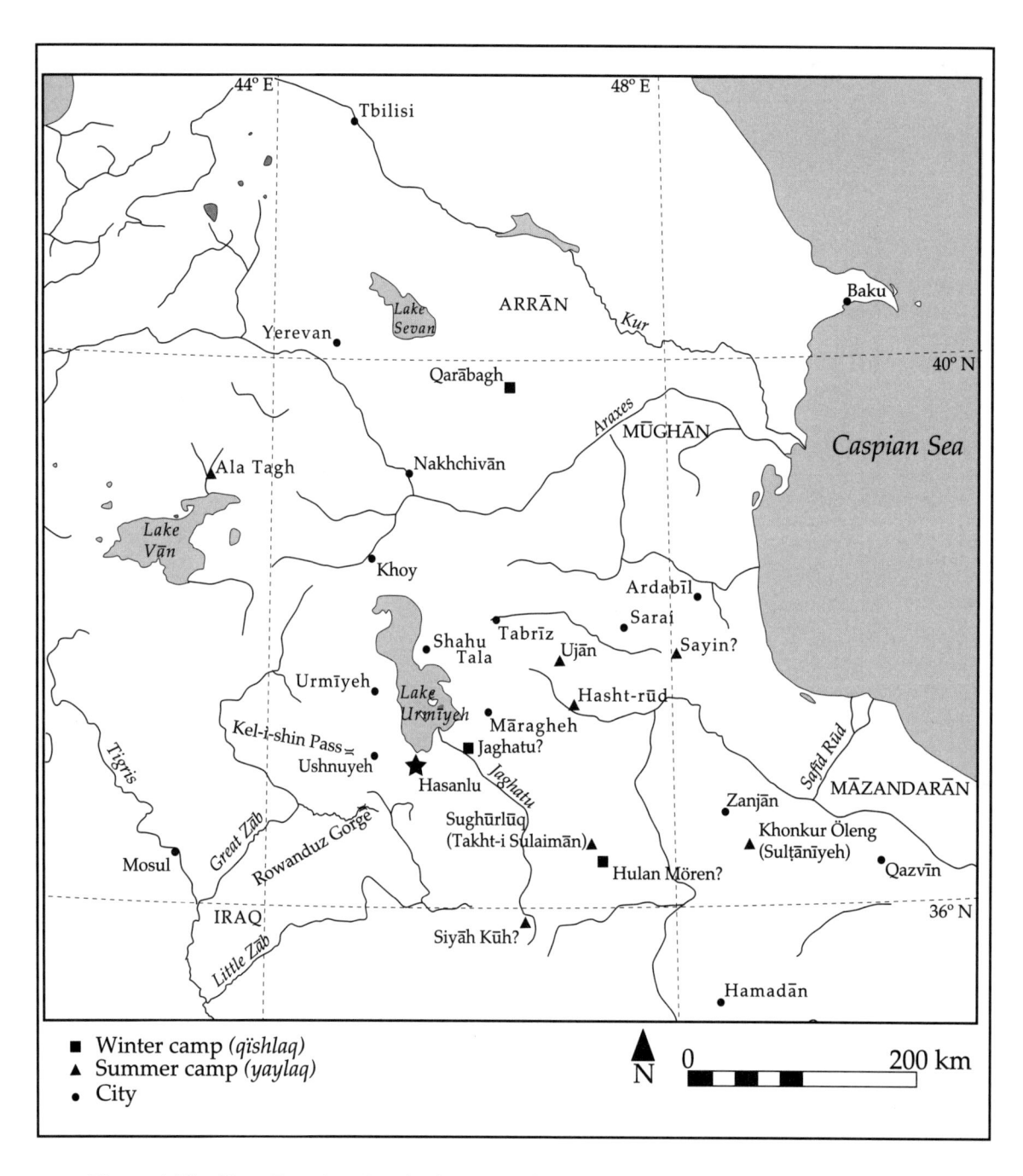

Figure 1. The Near East showing the location of Hasanlu Tepe and other Ilkhanid sites
(adapted from Masuya 2002:fig. 80).

1

Hasanlu Tepe and the Surrounding Area

The site of Hasanlu Tepe lies near the southern shore of Lake Urmīyeh in the Western Āzarbaijān Province of Iran (Figure 1). It is the largest ruin mound (*tepe*) in the Gadār River Valley, which runs from the western Zagros Mountains east to the marshy southern shore of Lake Urmīyeh (Figure 2). The western half of the valley is called Ushnu and the eastern, where Hasanlu is situated, Sūldūz.[*] Hasanlu lies in northeastern Sūldūz, in a basin surrounded by low hills. Small freshwater lakes, marshy areas that support fresh grasses even in the dry summer months, and a climate in which the plain remains nearly snow free in winter provide favorable conditions for herders as well as for a mixed farming and herding subsistence economy.

Hasanlu Tepe consists of a central High Mound, often called the "Citadel Mound" in preliminary reports, and a flanking Low Mound, dubbed the "Outer Town" (Figures 3 and 4). The High Mound rises 25 m above the surrounding plain, 27.5 m above the water table in 1960, and is 200 m in diameter. The Low Mound stands 8 m above sterile soil and measures 600 m across at its widest point, although its exact extent is obscured by the modern village of Hasanlu and recent agricultural activities (Plate A).

The modern village of Hasanlu, located just east of the High Mound, was founded sometime after the second Perso-Russian War (1826-28) following the Treaty of Turkomanchay. The inhabitants allegedly came from Georgia and speak the Karapapak (Eastern Anatolian) dialect of Azeri, the Turkic branch of the Altaic language family (Stein 1940:382). They were apparently settled at the border of Kurdistān in an attempt to stabilize the region. Today the Sūldūz area has a mosaic pattern of Kurdish and Turkish speaking villages.

The proximity of the village to the High Mound resulted in some minor disturbance to its uppermost levels, primarily in the form of trash pits and burials. No such remains were excavated in areas of the northern and eastern Low Mound that were tested. A canal, which separated the village from the site, cut the eastern edge of the Low Mound and often revealed ancient burials (Figure 3). The present-day village cemetery prevented excavation on a low rise in the southeastern Low Mound (Figures 3 and 4; Plate A).

Hasanlu was excavated by a joint expedition of the University of Pennsylvania Museum, the Metropolitan Museum of Art of New York, and the Archaeological Service of Iran under the direction of Robert H. Dyson, Jr. Between 1956 and 1977, the project completed 10 field seasons. The present volume is a final report on the excavated remains of Hasanlu Period I, which date approximately to the late 13th and 14th centuries AD.[†] This is the Ilkhanid period in northwestern Iran. At this time, one branch of the Mongol invaders who had wreaked so much devastation in western Asia and eastern Europe during the 13th century established

---

[*] For a full discussion of the surrounding region see Voigt (1983).

[†] See Dyson (1983:xxvii–xxviii) for a discussion of the complete Hasanlu sequence.

a semi-autonomous state centered on the area of modern Āzarbaijān and northwestern Iran. Several capital cities and palaces were located in the area of Lake Urmīyeh, indicative of the region's importance to the nomadic newcomers, who recognized the value of the region's lush summer pastures and its important overland routes, especially those leading west through the Zagros Mountains via the Kel-i Shin Pass and Rowanduz Pass to northern Iraq (Figure 1). To the southwest was another Ilkhanid capital city, Baghdad, the winter retreat of the Ilkhanid royal court. Farther west lay the unconquered lands of the Mamluks, the chief rivals of the new empire and the focus of many military campaigns.

Thus, it comes as no surprise that the archaeological record of Ushnu-Sūldūz, the western edge of the Ilkhanid heartland, reveals abundant evidence of Ilkhanid occupation, although archaeologists have devoted little attention to these important remains. Given the strategic and economic importance of the area, one would expect to find a fairly diverse range of Ilkhanid settlement types, ranging from seasonally utilized pastoral camps and small agricultural villages to fortified outposts, towns, and administrative centers. Hasanlu Tepe appears to have been a small planned, fortified settlement occupied year-round by a fairly prosperous populace. It is difficult to ascertain the site's function within the broader framework of the regional Ilkhanid settlement system given the limited archaeological dataset currently available for the region. However, the settlement's apparent importance relative to its small size was probably also linked to its proximity to the Mongol winter camp of Jaghatu (Figure 1).

This report is organized by the relevant excavation areas, including the southern, northwestern, and northeastern highpoints of the High Mound (three of the four crests on the High Mound), and the northern stratigraphic trench (Operations I and VII, see below). These excavation areas are presented separately since they were noncontiguous exposures of separate, isolated Period I buildings; that is, they were not architecturally or stratigraphically linked. Therefore, there will always be some questions regarding the exact chronological cross sequencing of these areas, but all probably date to within a single century based on similarities in the respective ceramic assemblages.

The attribution of the various deposits to Period I was based on similarities in glazed ceramics, plain wares, and architecture (in order of ascribed importance). There were no means for obtaining calendric dates for Period I: no radiocarbon samples were collected from Period I deposits, and no datable inscriptions or coins, other than surface finds of the 19th century, were found.

In some areas of the site where architectural remains and features lay near the surface, it has been extremely difficult to assign them to any given period due to the poor preservation of near-surface architecture and a paucity of associated diagnostic artifacts. In this regard, documenting the modern surface conditions of the High Mound prior to the excavations, using aerial photographs, excavation notes, and ethnohistoric accounts, has proven particularly useful, providing a supporting line of evidence for the attribution of features and architecture to Period I. When the spatial extent of a polygonal soil discoloration on the surface of the High Mound was mapped using aerial photos and combined with topographic maps and the Period I architectural plans and sections, it revealed what is almost certainly a poorly preserved Period I circumvallation (see below). The surface soil discoloration enclosed all the stratified Period I deposits and Period I architecture was always aligned to it. In the few places where Period I strata were not severely eroded, the surface feature was usually associated with poorly preserved subsurface remains such as walls and possibly a ditch.

It should be pointed out that the latter part of the Hasanlu sequence—Periods IIIB, IIIA/II, and I—was recovered in an unbroken stratigraphic sequence only on the southern High Mound (see below, Buildings I and II). In most of the excavation areas on the High Mound, the first intact occupational remains encountered dated to Period IIIB.

This volume also includes a brief report on a few sites with proven or potential Period I occupations in northern Iran recorded by the Hasanlu Project during archaeological reconnaissance, surveys, and excavations. The difficulties of distinguishing late Saljūq remains from those of the early Ilkhanid are examined with regard to ceramic assemblages gathered during archaeological surveys.

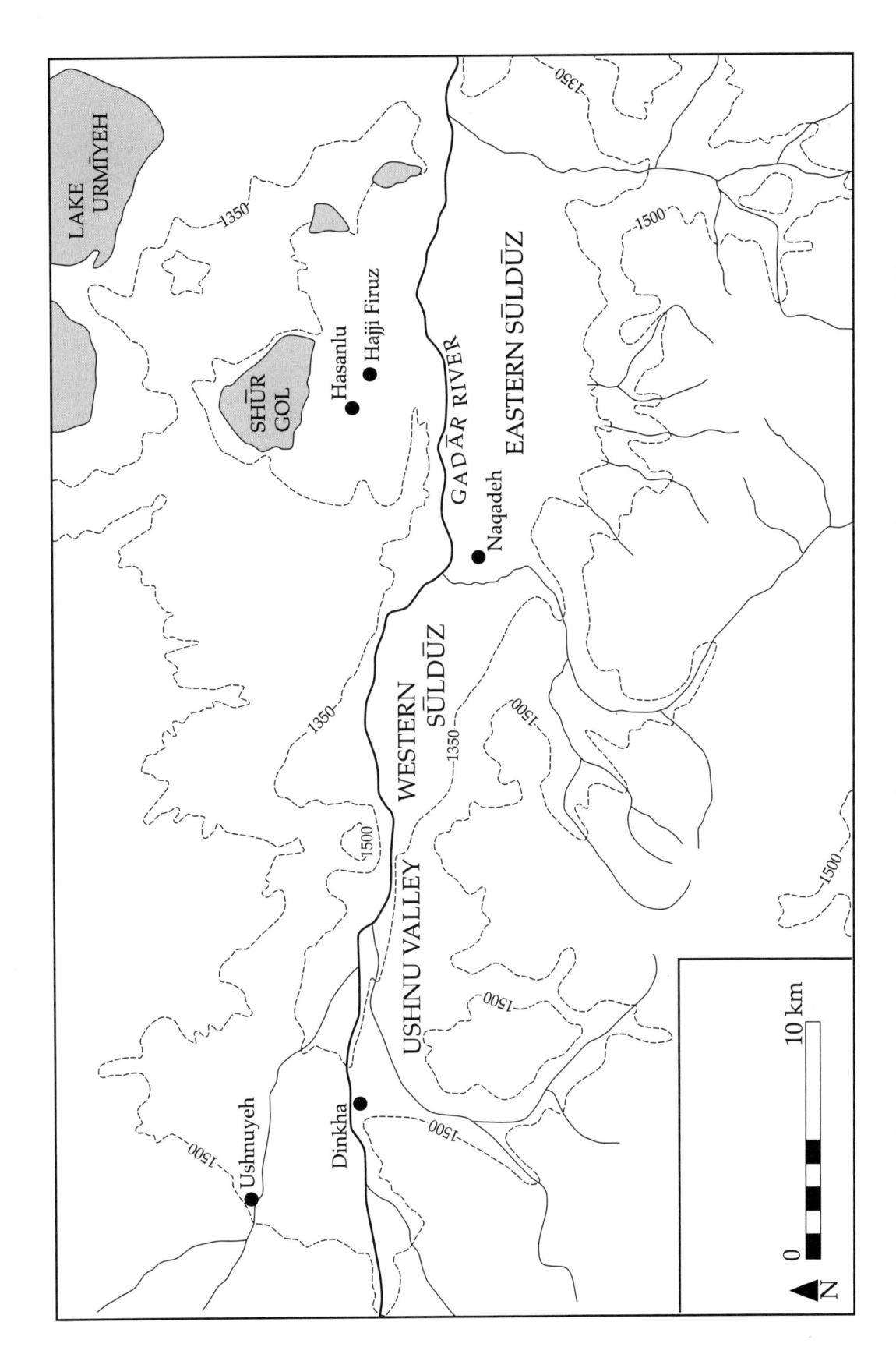

Figure 2. The Ushnu-Sūldūz valley showing the location of Hasanlu Tepe and other sites of the Saljūq and Ilkhanid Periods.

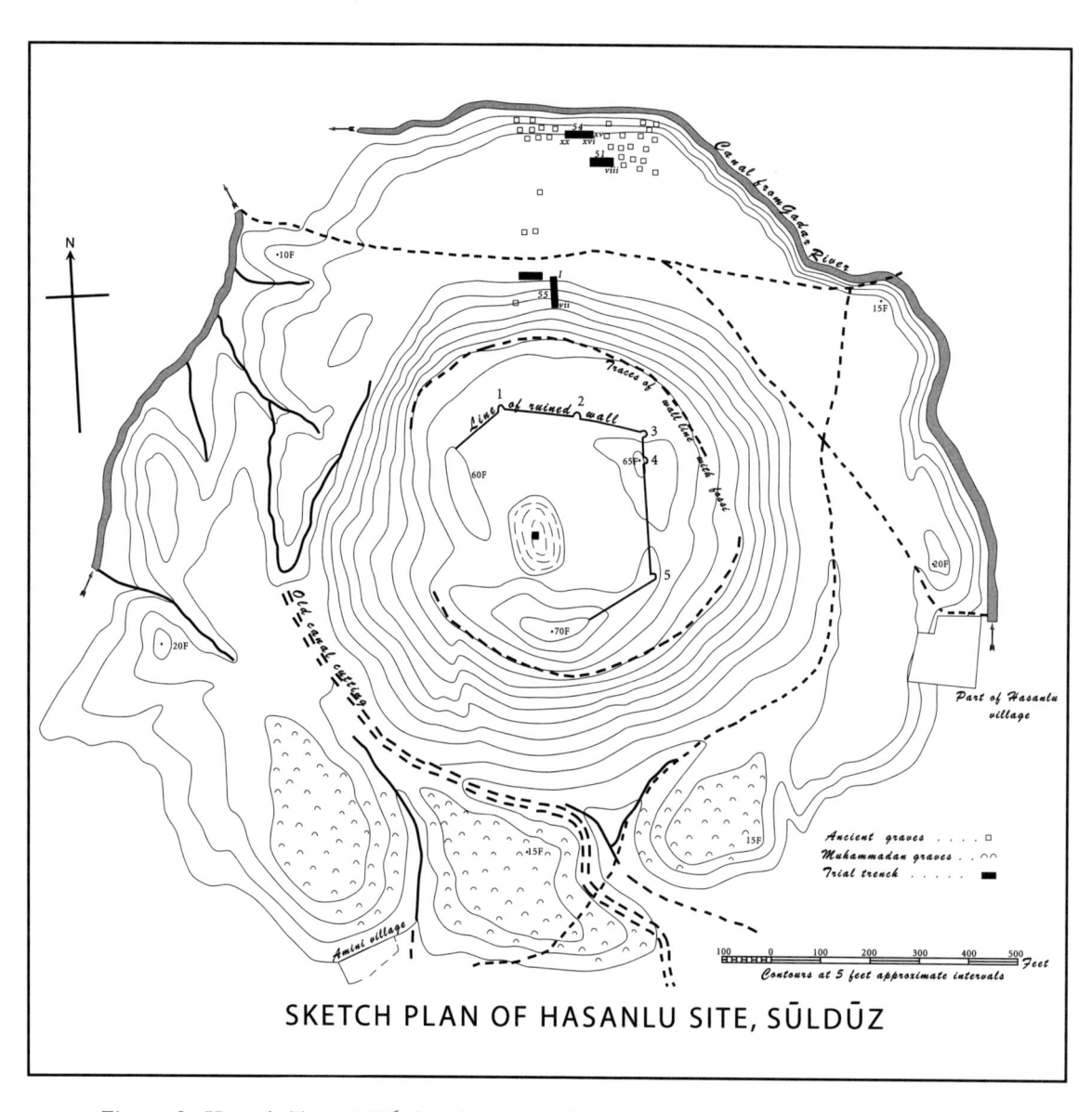

Figure 3. Hasanlu Tepe: 1936 sketch map by Sir Aurel Stein (adapted from Stein 1940).

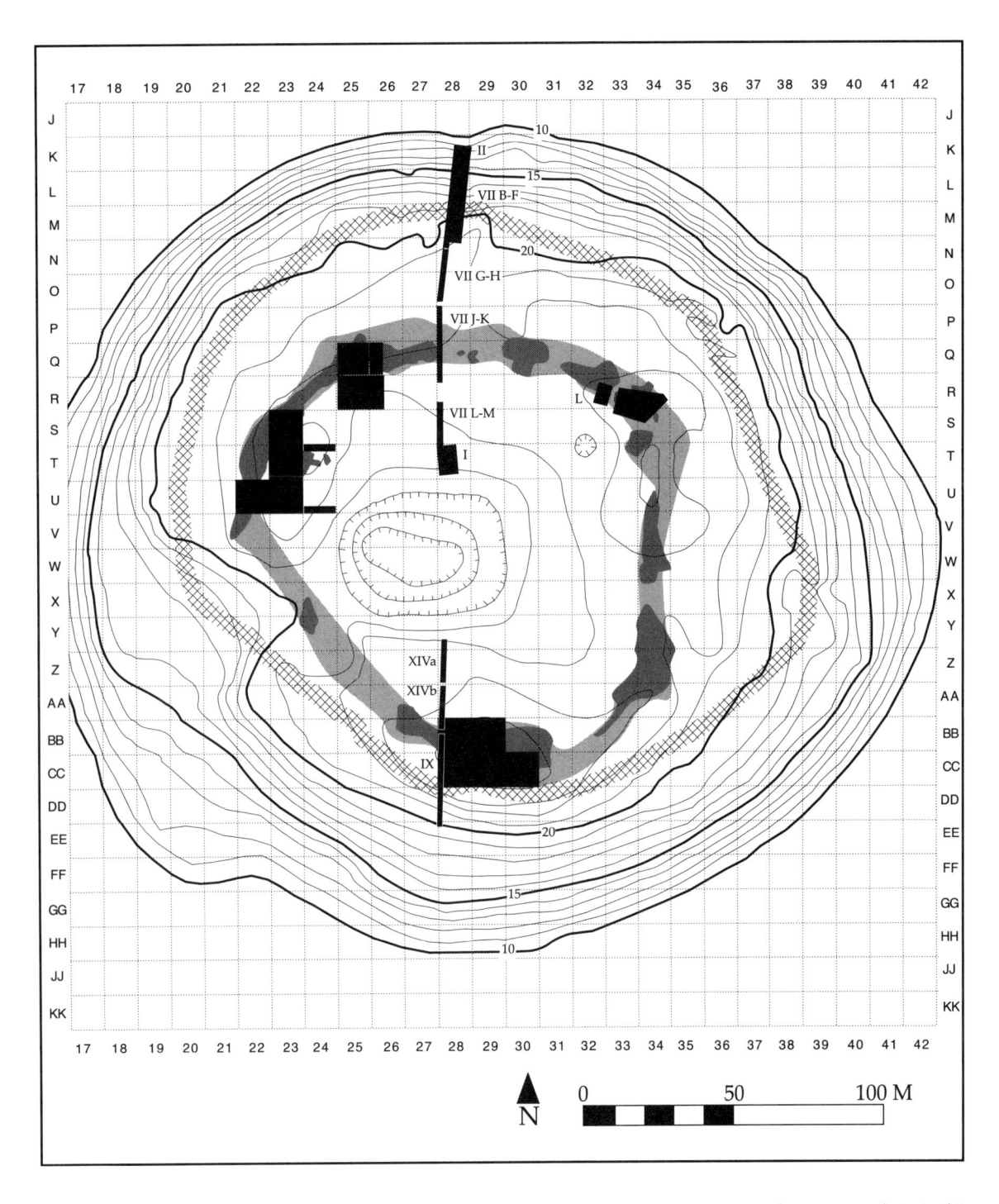

Figure 4. Hasanlu Tepe: Topographic plan of the High Mound showing areas with excavated Period I architecture (black), the surface soil discoloration visible on aerial photographs (grays), and the modern military trench (crosshatching). Contour interval 1m, grid of 11m squares.

2

HISTORY OF THE EXCAVATION OF PERIOD I, 1956–62

Maḥmūd Rād and a Mr. Farhādī carried out the first excavations at Hasanlu for commercial purposes in 1934-35 (Ghirshman 1939:78-79, 253-254, pl. C; Mostafavi 1960). Artifacts collected through commercial excavations were sold on the antiquities market. Rād and Farhādī's work was confined to the northeastern Low Mound. In 1936, Sir Aurel Stein spent six days excavating four trenches, two on the northern Low Mound, an L-shaped trench at the base of the High Mound's northern slope, and a sounding in the High Mound's central depression (Figure 3, Plate A; Stein 1940:389-404, figs. 106, 108-110; pls. XXIV-XXVI, XXX-XXXI). Material from these excavations was divided between the British Museum and Tehran. 'Alī Ḥākemī and Maḥmūd Rād resumed commercial excavations on the east edge of the Low Mound in 1947 and 1949, opening a number of graves (Ḥākemī and Rād 1950). None of these early excavations uncovered Period I strata.

Apart from Stein's sounding in the central depression, the High Mound, the area of the Period I occupation, was not excavated until 1956. Dyson was aware of post-Iron Age occupation on top of the *tepe* prior to the 1956 excavations based on surface finds of glazed pottery and the published accounts of earlier visitors and excavators. Stein had mapped the lines of architectural remains on the High Mound's surface, including what he interpreted as a late fortification wall (Figure 3; Stein 1940:379, Sketch Plan 25; 391-92). The remains of this inner circumvallation appear clearly on a low-level aerial photo taken in 1937 by Erich F. Schmidt (Plate A) as a polygonal soil discoloration, measuring 132 m in diameter and enclosing approximately 1.4 ha. The line of the Iron Age city wall—the outer circumvallation—and a circular military trench dug prior to 1937 also appear on the photograph (Dyson 1959:9).* This military trench was probably dug during World War I by Turkish or, more likely, Russian forces and generally followed the line of the Iron Age (Period IIIB) city wall.

The 1956–62 excavations defined the limits of Period I occupation as the area of the High Mound lying within the soil discoloration visible on the mound's surface and in aerial photographs. No substantial stratified Period I remains were uncovered in subsequent excavations. Overall, Period I levels were often badly eroded and were relatively thin, averaging 60 cm in depth in the best-preserved portions of the *tepe*.

In 1956, Dyson undertook a four-month reconnaissance of sites in northern Iran (Dyson 1956, 1957). Ten days were spent excavating at Hasanlu on the High Mound (Operations I-III, Grids T28, L28, and W26/27) (Figure 4; Dyson 1956). In Operation I, located north of a depression at the center of the High Mound, excavations revealed what were initially interpreted as "two paved 'Islamic' stairways" (Dyson 1956:284). These were later re-dated to the Iron Age (Dyson 1957:38), but upon further review we now believe they date to Period I (see below).

---

* Aerial photograph dated July 25, 1937, provided to Dyson by Erich F. Schmidt (negative, Oriental Institute AE 650).

Over the course of the succeeding excavation seasons at Hasanlu, the excavators' understanding of the regional archaeological sequence and of the site's morphology would improve exponentially. So too would techniques for excavation and recording in Near Eastern archaeology in general, and these advances were quickly adopted, and some developed, at Hasanlu. Moreover, as the expedition became more experienced with the hardships and logistical challenges involved in carrying out large-scale excavations in a remote, archaeologically unknown region, the overall quality and efficiency of the work improved. For these reasons, there is a higher degree of detail and reliability in the excavation records from later seasons, especially from the period from 1970 onward. In terms of Period I deposits, most of these exposures were completed in the early years of digging, and so have occasionally presented some challenges with regard to interpretation. Moreover, the Period I remains often lay at or just below the surface and so were often disturbed or nearly eroded away. Thus, they often were absent or possibly went unnoticed as the turf and topsoil were removed in preparation for controlled stratigraphic excavation. The primary objective of most of the excavation areas was to increase horizontal exposures of the sacked and burned Hasanlu IVB city and the later Urartian IIIB fortress; later periods were of secondary importance.

A complete topographic map of the site was completed in 1970 using a planing table. Prior to this, several partial topographic maps of the High Mound showing excavation areas were drawn using a planing table. Different control points/mapping stations were usually used each season for the mapping, introducing a potential source of error in spatial control and making it virtually impossible to use one system of absolute elevations for the excavated remains across the entire site.

Excavation procedures varied from season to season. From 1958 onward, excavation units were usually 11 x 11 m squares with 0.5 m balks, so the excavated area was 10 x 10 m. Prior to this, excavation units were laid out according to excavation objectives, terrain, and the time and resources available. Balks were usually removed following the completion of the excavations of Period IVB, and sections were frequently not drawn. The excavation supervisors usually drew plans at various scales of architecture and other features following the completion of a coherent architectural phase. Photography was used fairly extensively during the excavations, both for recording excavation areas and artifactual finds.

Excavation supervisors, usually graduate students, were put in charge of one or more excavation units, which were excavated by crews of varying size. Notes were usually taken at the completion of each major architectural phase in the 1956-62 seasons. In a few cases, notes were taken on a daily basis and were dated. In some instances, there are no notes for excavation areas. Sieving was not employed in the early seasons and botanical and faunal remains were not systematically collected.

There was no single system used for the collection and recording of ceramics. In the 1956-62 seasons, nondiagnostic bodysherds were seldom collected, and often only decorated wares (e.g., glazed, painted, incised) and whole vessels were collected/recorded from Period I-IIIA deposits (see below).

Between 1956 and 1962, excavation units called Operations were given Operation Numbers designated by roman numerals. In 1962, the project switched from using Operation Numbers to the use of Grid Designations, which refer to 11 x 11 m squares designated by alphabetical and numerical axes. This grid system covered the entire site (Figure 4). The 11 m square was adopted so that the actual digging area was 10 by 10 m with 0.5 m balks, making recording easier. Within excavation areas, stratigraphic units were given Stratum Numbers—usually the only means of vertical control used for the recording of finds. Area Numbers were employed for horizontal control. Areas usually correspond to rooms and occasionally the interior of other features such as pits and burials. Artifacts from an excavation area were given an Object Number in the field by the excavation supervisor. Stratum, Area, and Object Numbers are only unique within a given Operation. Artifacts were later given a unique Hasanlu Number, also called the Field Number, designated by a prefix consisting of the abbreviation "HAS" followed by the last two digits of the excavation year, which was followed by a hyphen and a numerical identifier (e.g., HAS 58-242). Occasionally, these numbers were later subdivided by alphabetic designations (e.g., Has 58-232a, b).

Exploratory work continued at Hasanlu in 1957-58. The 1957 excavations on the High Mound focused on connecting Operation I to Operation II and Operation II to Stein's north-slope trench, thereby sectioning the northern High Mound (Dyson 1958a:128, 1958b:32). This was accomplished with a trench 62 m long by 1.7 m wide (including balks) designated Operation VII (Figure 4; Grids S28-M28). The trench revealed Period I walls and associated features, including a "mediaeval Islamic fortification wall" (Dyson 1958a:128). The trench penetrated Period I strata only on its north end, where it also revealed the Iron Age fortification wall (Fortification Wall II) of Period IIIB. The expedition also opened Operations IV-VI on the northeastern Low Mound (Grids S48-49; Q42-3, R43-44; F38-39), but found no stratified Period I remains there. However, surface finds in the area of an orchard south of Hasanlu revealed Islamic period occupation roughly contemporary to Hasanlu Period I.*

In 1958, the expedition extended the line of Operation VII across the southern High Mound with Operations XIV (Grid Y27/28 to BB27/28) and IX (Figure 4; Grid BB27 to EE27). Work also continued near the central depression of the High Mound in Operation VIII (Grid T27). The 1958 season also saw the first attempts to clear large areas of the southwestern High Mound (Operations XX-XXIX; Grids Y25-27, Z25-27, AA25-27). Operations V and X (Grid A28-B28) continued work in the eastern and northern Low Mound.

Virtually no Period I material was found during this season, although the horizontal exposure on the southwestern High Mound was situated over a segment of the heavily eroded Period I fortification visible on aerial photographs. The north end of Operation IX revealed a short east-west segment of the Period I fortifications—a poorly preserved mud-brick wall later found to be entirely eroded away only a short distance northwest of Operation IX in Grid BB27 (Figures 5 and 9). The wall was preserved four courses high at its east end and built of square bricks measuring 22 x 22 x 5-8 cm. This was the standard brick size during Period I. The excavation also traced a long segment of the southern Iron Age fortification wall of Period IIIB (Operations IXR and IXL), and searched for this fortification on the mound's eastern slope using a series of radial trenches numbered Operations XI (Grids X37-39), XII (Grids P37-38, Q37-38), and XIII (Grid CC36).

In 1959, following the famous discoveries made in the Iron Age burned buildings of Hasanlu Period IVB in 1958 (Dyson 1959; Porada 1959, 1967), Operations XXII-XXV were continued and new excavation areas were laid out to clear a larger area of the southwestern High Mound (Dyson 1960), Operations XV-XIX (Grids BB27-DD27, BB26-CC26), XXX (Grid Y24), XXXIX (Grid BB28), XLII (Grid AA28), XLIV (Grid Z29), XLV (Grid Z28), XLVII (Grid Y28), and XLVIII (Grid 29). During this season, the excavations uncovered the first substantial Period I architectural remains on the southern High Mound in Operation XXXIX (Grid BB28). The excavations also continued the work of tracing Fortification Wall II (Period IIIB) and opened stratigraphic trenches across the mound's western and southern slopes—Operations XXXA (Grids Y21-23, Z21-22) and XXXIIIA (Grids EE28-GG 28), respectively. On the northeastern corner of the High Mound, the excavators laid out two irregularly shaped excavation areas to trace the putative Period I fortification (Operation L, Grids R32-34, S33-34). They found no traces of the fortification, but cleared two building phases of a single room, probably part of a larger Period I house (see Building V below). As in previous seasons, work continued on the Low Mound in Operations LI-LIV (Grids B28-29, C28-29, D29-30, E30; NN30-OO30; L11; B29-30, C30-31, D31-32, respectively) and in extensions of Operations V and VI.

The 1960 season expanded the horizontal clearance of Iron Age remains on the southern High Mound (Dyson 1961), Operations XXXI-XXXVIII (Grids DD28-30, CC28-30, BB29-30), XL (Grid AA30), XLIII (Grid Z30), LXXVII (Grid X29), LXXVIII (Grid X28), LXXX (Grid W28), LXXXII (Grid W29); Operations XXXIX and XLVIII were continued. Operations XXXV (CC29), XXXVI (CC28), and XXXVIII (BB29) revealed the entire Period I house first found in 1959, and Operation XXXIV (CC30)

---

* Dyson Field Journal (1957). Dyson noted the presence of a "bowl fragment of iridescent greenish glass," an "'egg' of white iridescent glass (probably a perfume bottle)," and "plain ware sherds and incised sherds like those on top of the main mound," as well as "burned rectangular bricks."

uncovered an adjacent structure (see Buildings I and II below). The excavators also continued Operation XXXA on the western slope of the High Mound.

In 1962, the expedition cleared most of the High Mound's northwest corner (Grids O23-24, P22-24, Q23-26, R20-26, S22-26, T22-24, and U21-24). This area contained parts of two stratified Period I buildings (see Buildings III and IV below). The excavators also continued work on the mound's western slope (Grids V23, W20, X20-23, Y21) and extended the exposure of Iron Age remains on the southern High Mound (AA31, BB31, and CC31).

3

THE SOUTHERN HIGH MOUND

OPERATIONS IX, XXXIV–XXXVI, XXXVIII–XXXIX
GRIDS BB28–29, CC28–30

In 1958-60, the excavators uncovered stratified Period I remains over an area of 605 m² on the highest point of the southern High Mound. The structures included a single house (Building I), consisting of six rooms surrounding a central court and what is likely an adjoining tower (Building II) (Figure 5). Building I was constructed of thin, square mudbricks (bricks measured 23 x 23 x 8 cm). Each brick bears three diagonal grooves made by fingertips drawn across their top while the brick was wet—a feature still seen on modern bricks of the same size in the area. The walls were set on mudbrick footings four bricks in width. The faces of the footings were preserved 5-10 cm beyond the walls on either side. The walls, preserved from 44 to 120 cm high, were centered over the footings and were three bricks wide. The northern walls of the building were set in wall trenches cut into Period II Stratum 3 (Figure 7).

All rooms had two plastered floor levels; later structural modifications rested on fills that had accumulated on Floor 1 (Figure 7). The two phases of Building II were preserved largely as stone footings and abutted Building I on its east side (Plate 2). The southern footing of the later phase had eroded away (Figure 5).

BUILDING I (FIGURE 5)

OPERATIONS XXXIV–XXXVI, XXXVIII–XXXIX
GRIDS BB28–29, CC28–30

Room 1 (5.18 x 4.97 m), the central court, contained no artifacts or features of note (Figure 5).* This court lay below the level of the surrounding rooms and was probably not roofed.

Room 2 (4.23 x 5.05 m) apparently formed part of the court at one point, but was later partitioned by an unbonded, two-brick-wide wall preserved only 60 cm in height. No doorway was preserved in this wall. Floor 1 passed under this wall and Floor 2 ran against it (Figure 7). Room 2 was missing its southern wall, which was either eroded away or cut by the modern military trench.

Room 3 (5.79 x 3.62 m) at the southwestern corner of the building contained no artifacts or features. The room was connected to the central court by a doorway (width 90 cm) with a raised threshold of mudbrick built on Floor 1 and sealed by Floor 2. The southern end of this room was also eroded or cut away.

Room 4 (4.83 x 3.59 m), north of Room 3, had a door (width 97 cm) with a mudbrick sill standing 10 cm above Floor 2. The room contained an oven made from a buff ware ceramic vessel missing its rim and sunk 65 cm below Floor 1 (Plates D and

---

* All room measurements are of internal space.

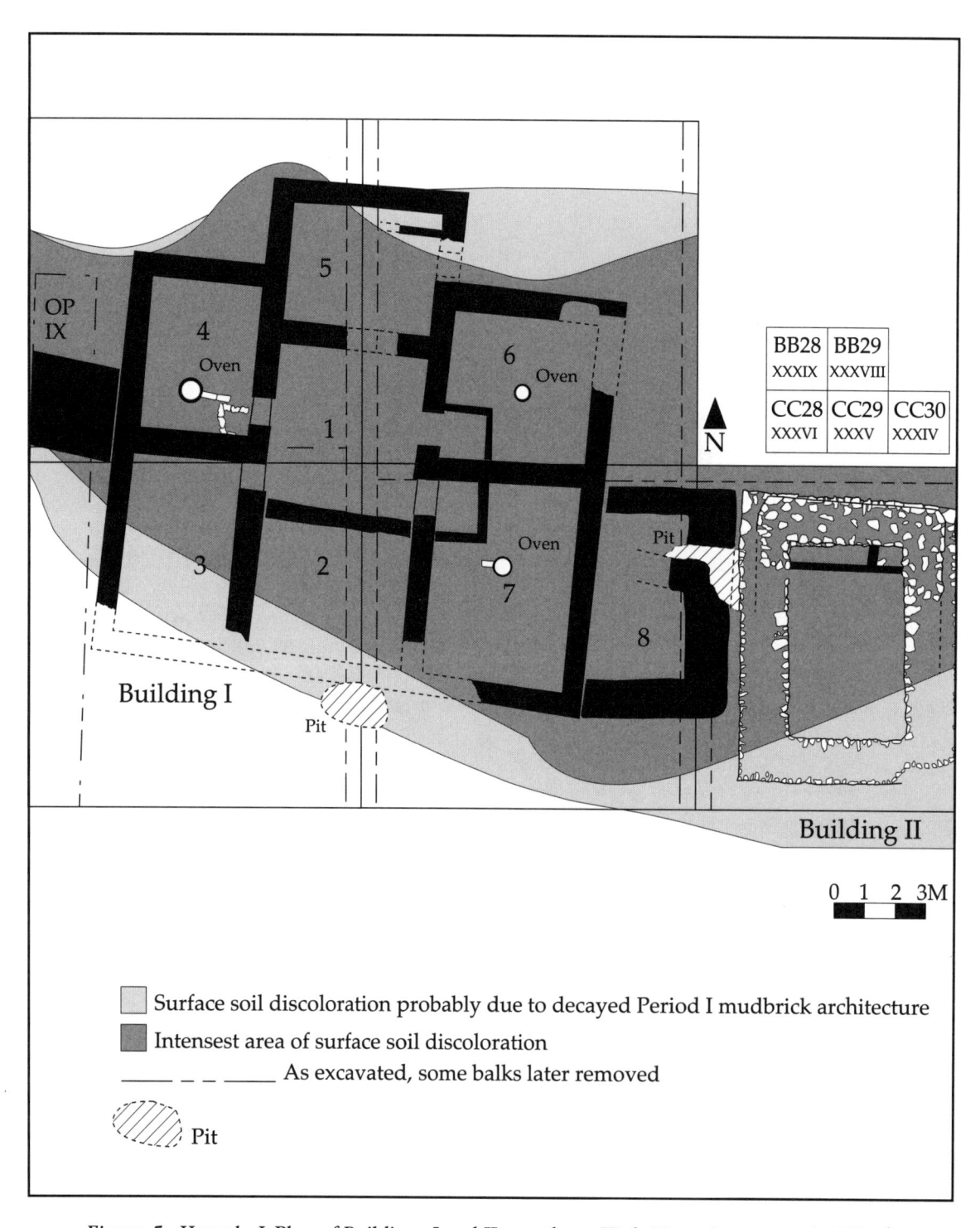

Figure 5. Hasanlu I: Plan of Buildings I and II, southern High Mound, excavated 1958-60.

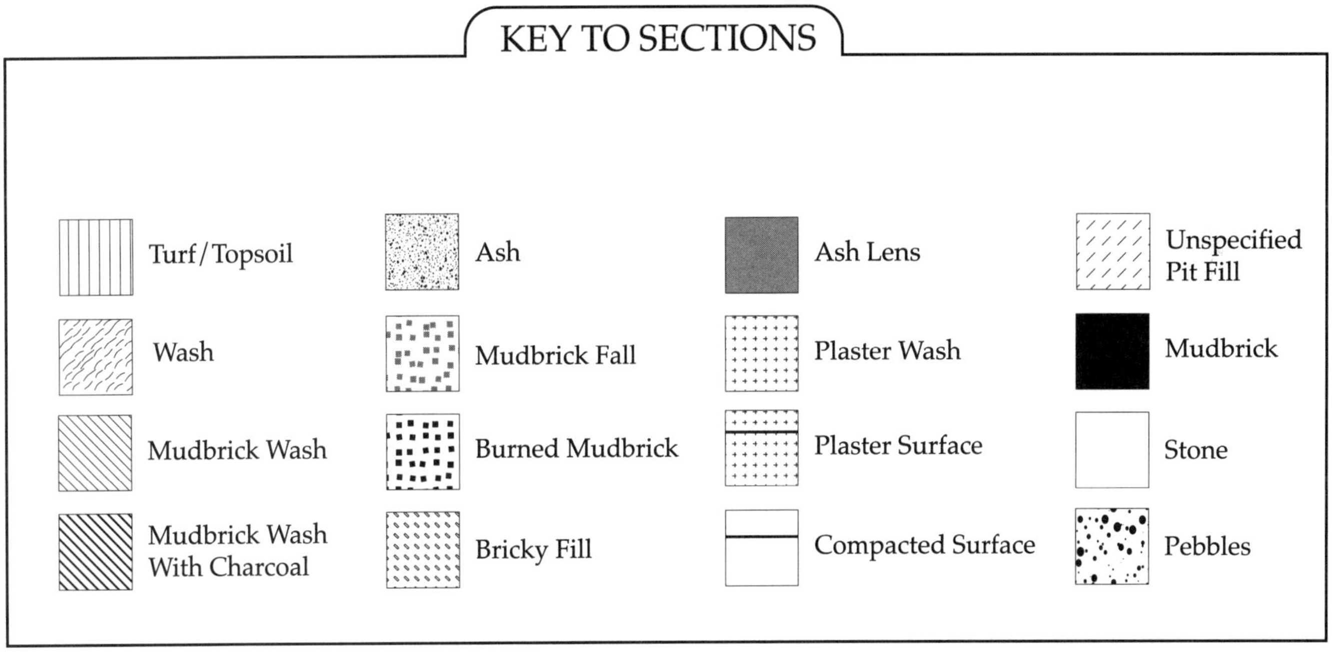

KEY TO SECTIONS

Turf/Topsoil	Ash	Ash Lens	Unspecified Pit Fill
Wash	Mudbrick Fall	Plaster Wash	Mudbrick
Mudbrick Wash	Burned Mudbrick	Plaster Surface	Stone
Mudbrick Wash With Charcoal	Bricky Fill	Compacted Surface	Pebbles

Figure 6. Key to sections.

E). The oven had a flue consisting of two ceramic pipe segments (HAS 59-647a, b) together measuring 47.5 cm long, each with rim diameters of 16 cm on one end and 10 cm on the other (Figure 8). The flue was 45 cm below the oven's rim and sloped up to the floor levels. In the southeast corner of the room, the excavators noted a deep organic deposit surrounded by stones, which they interpreted as a chicken coop (Plate F). Alternatively, this area might have been used to store dung fuel. A mudbrick fortification wall approximately 3 m wide abutted Rooms 3 and 4 on the west (Figure 9).

Room 5 (3.92 x 4.91 m) at the north end of the court appears to have served as the entrance chamber to the building with a doorway opening to the east (Figure 5). Both jambs of this doorway were damaged, so the width of the main entrance could not be determined. There were two distinct floor levels separated by a layer of collapsed brick and brickbats fallen from the room's north wall (Figure 7, Stratum 2b). Examination of the north wall's masonry revealed the existence of a cut line separating the original brickwork from a later rebuild. Floor 2, associated with the rebuild of the north wall, lay 44 cm above Floor 1, or 28 cm above the contemporary Floor 2 in the court. Presumably one stepped down into the central court from Room 5, although no steps were found. At the north end of the room, there was a low, narrow wall (width 28 cm) forming a bin along the north wall (Figure 5). Modern bins of this type commonly hold animal feed.

Room 6 (4.62 x 4.74 m) on the northeast side of the court contained a circular ceramic oven, which measured 58 cm in depth and 55 cm in diameter. At the entrance to the room, a rectangular area lay 30 cm below the room's floor (the same level as the courtyard) and was lined with mudbricks.

Room 7 (6.41 x 4.69 m), south of Room 6, contained a ceramic oven 50 cm in diameter and sunk 60 cm below floor level. Beneath the floor, the hearth had a two-segment ceramic flue, measuring 95 cm in length and 16 cm in diameter. The flue sloped up to the floor level. The door (width 92 cm) had a mudbrick threshold, which opened onto a sunken rectangular area 30 cm below floor level and lined with mudbricks. The excavators noted the presence of mud plaster on the interior wall faces of the room. The only small find reported for Building I is a stone bead found in Room 7 (Figure 12:1).

Room 8 (5.29 x 2.83 m) to the southeast was founded on the same level as Building I Floor 2, and thus dates to the structure's second phase (Figure 10). Its walls abutted the house's west wall, but were not bonded to it, showing that it was a secondary addition. The walls, preserved 60 cm high and 88 to 134 cm wide, were of packed mud (*tauf*) rather than mudbrick and were aligned slightly oblique to the walls of Building I. The remains of an east-west interior wall, found only in the section, were badly damaged by a later burial. Room 8 may have filled the space between Phase 2 of Buildings I and II, forming part of the fortification system. A gap of at least 4.72 m might have existed between the two buildings in Phase 1.

BUILDING II (FIGURE 5)

OPERATION XXXIV
GRID CC30

This structure, preserved in two separate phases, probably served as a tower in the fortification system (Plate G). All that remained of the structure were stone rubble footings and thin, interior mudbrick walls, possibly a bin. The footings were preserved from 20 to 60 cm high, depending on the surface slope of the *tepe*.

The earlier Phase 1 footings were 1.50 to 1.60 m wide and the rubble was bound together using a mud mortar. The northern end of the building was set in a wall trench (Building II lay outside Operation CC30's balks, and thus is not recorded in any sections). The Phase 1 structure was contemporary to the earlier of two clay-paved exterior surfaces, both of which ran against the east wall of Building I Rooms 6 and 7, which also rested in a wall trench (Figure 11, Surfaces 1 and 2, Stratum 2a). Phase 1 of Building I and Phase 1 of Building II were probably contemporary, although the question remains unresolved based on the available evidence.

The first phase of Building II was eventually leveled, and a new, smaller structure was built in its place. Only the north end of this structure was preserved. The new structure followed the interior lines of the Phase 1 footings, but the exterior faces of the

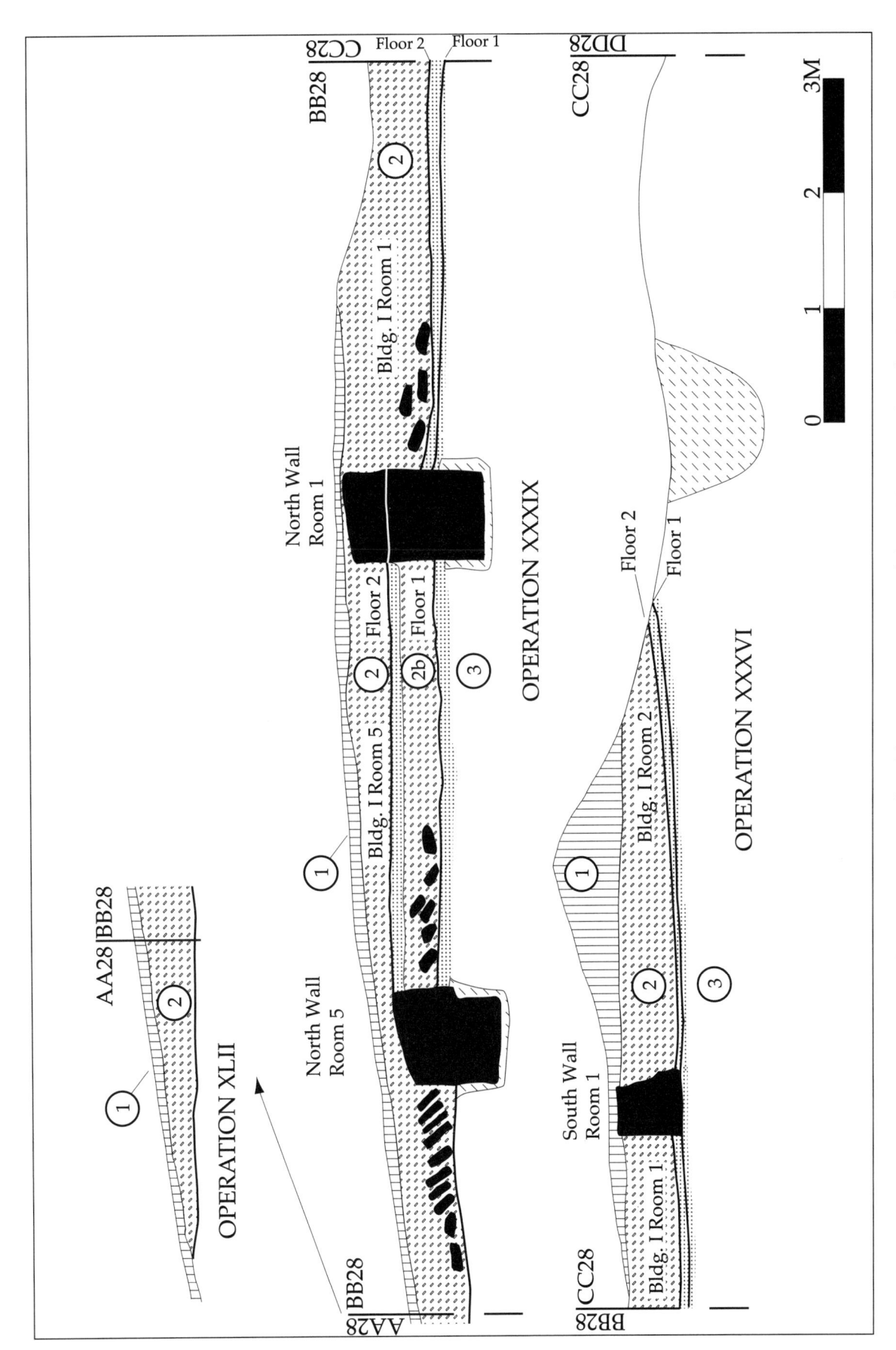

Figure 7. Hasanlu I: East section of Building I, Rooms 1, 2, and 5 (AA29-DD28). See Plan, Fig 5.

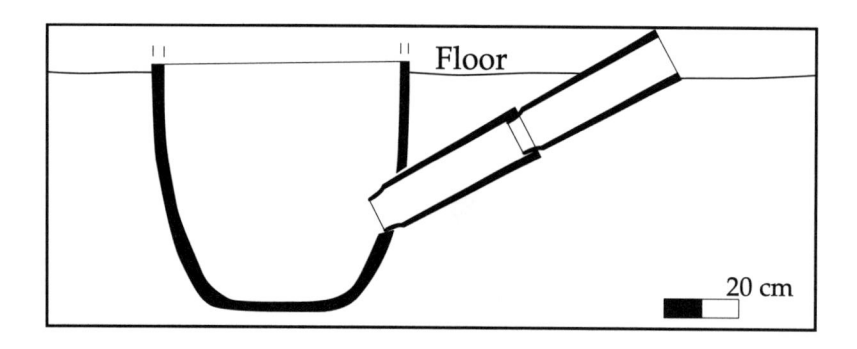

Figure 8. Hasanlu I: East-west section through oven and flue segments (HAS 59-647) in Building I, Room 4 (BB28). See plan, Fig. 5.

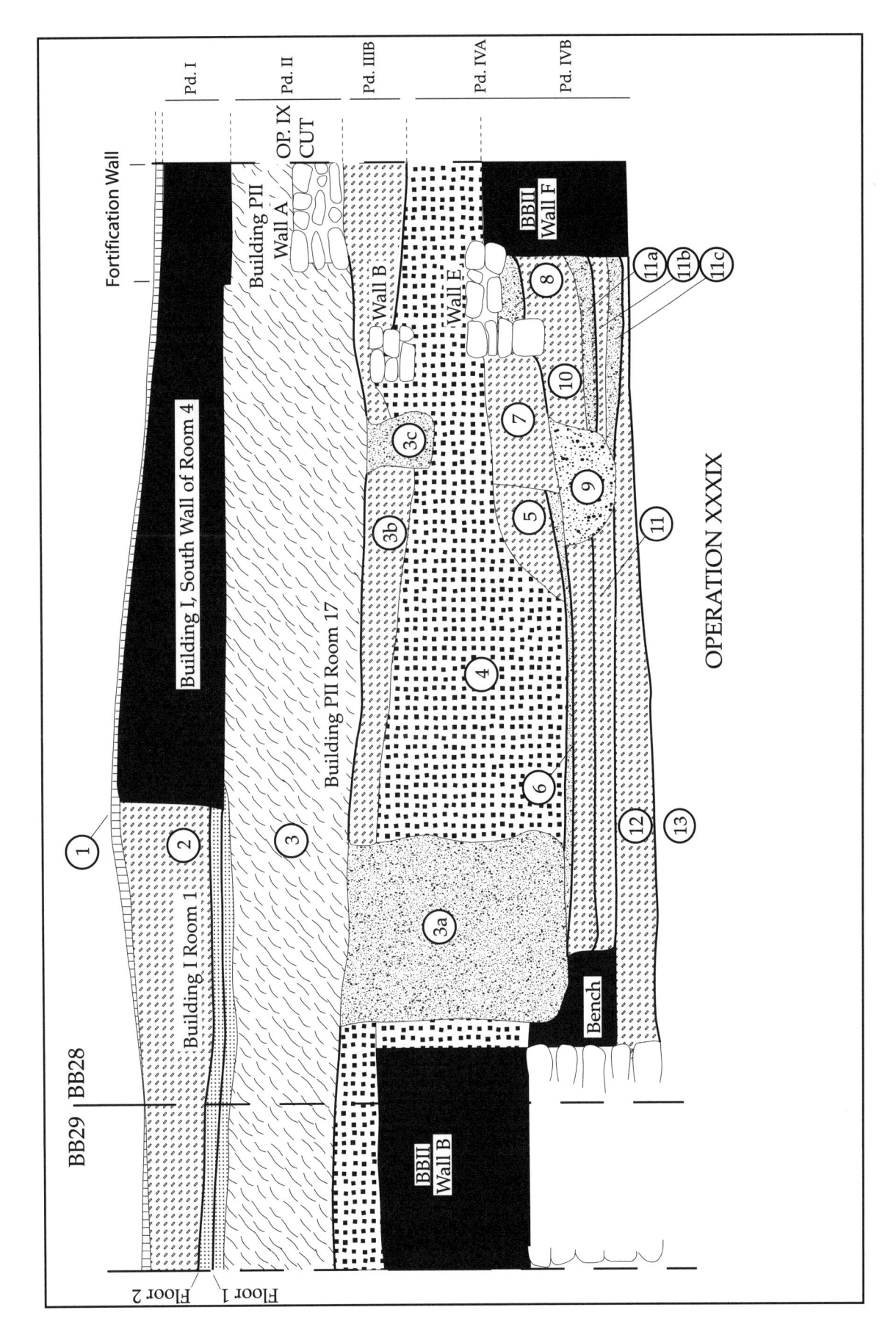

Figure 9. Hasanlu I: South section of Building I, Rooms 1 and 4 (BB28-BB29), showing its relationship to strata of Periods II-IVB. See plan, Fig. 5.

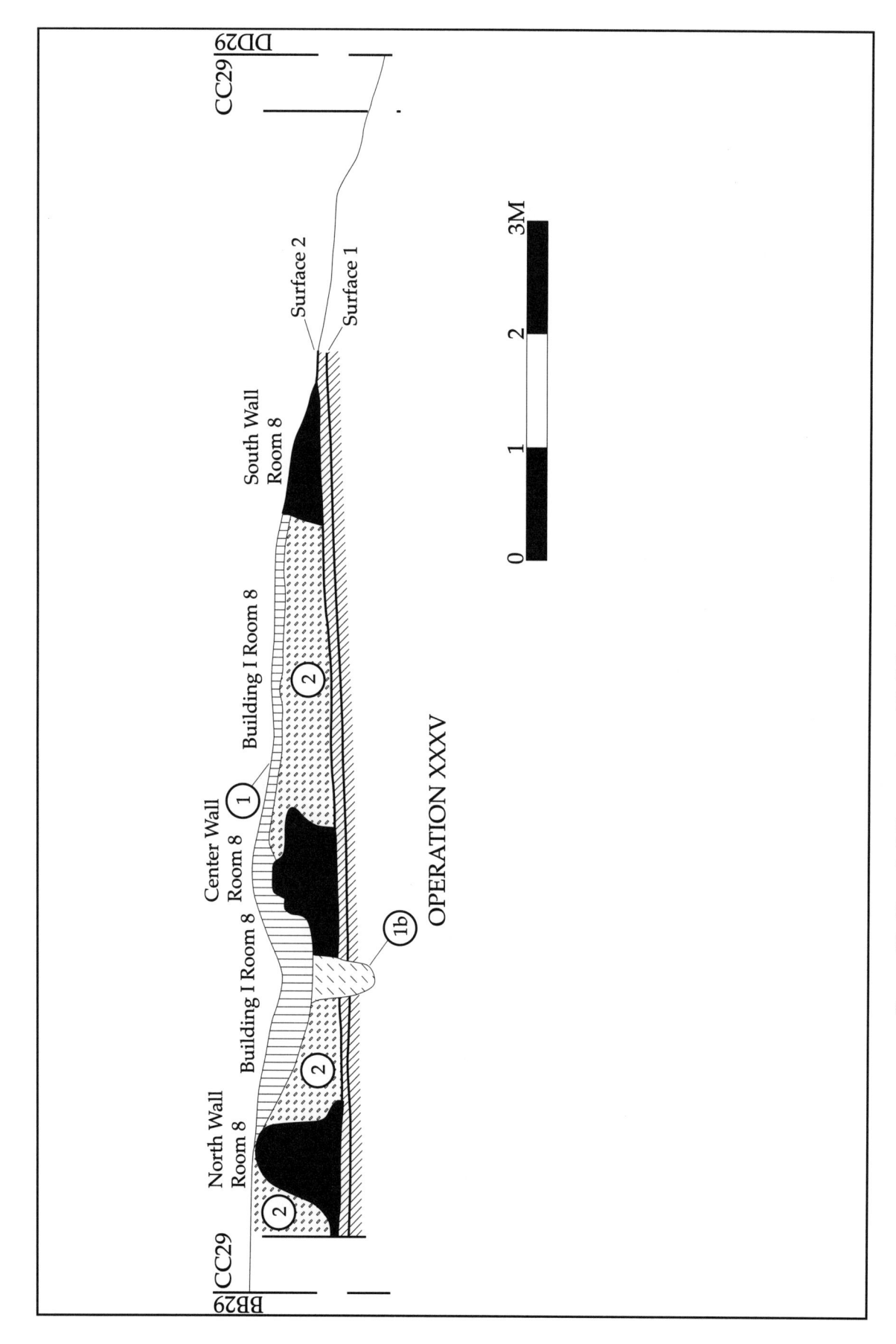

Figure 10. Hasanlu I: East section of Building I, Room 8 (CC29). See plan, Fig. 5.

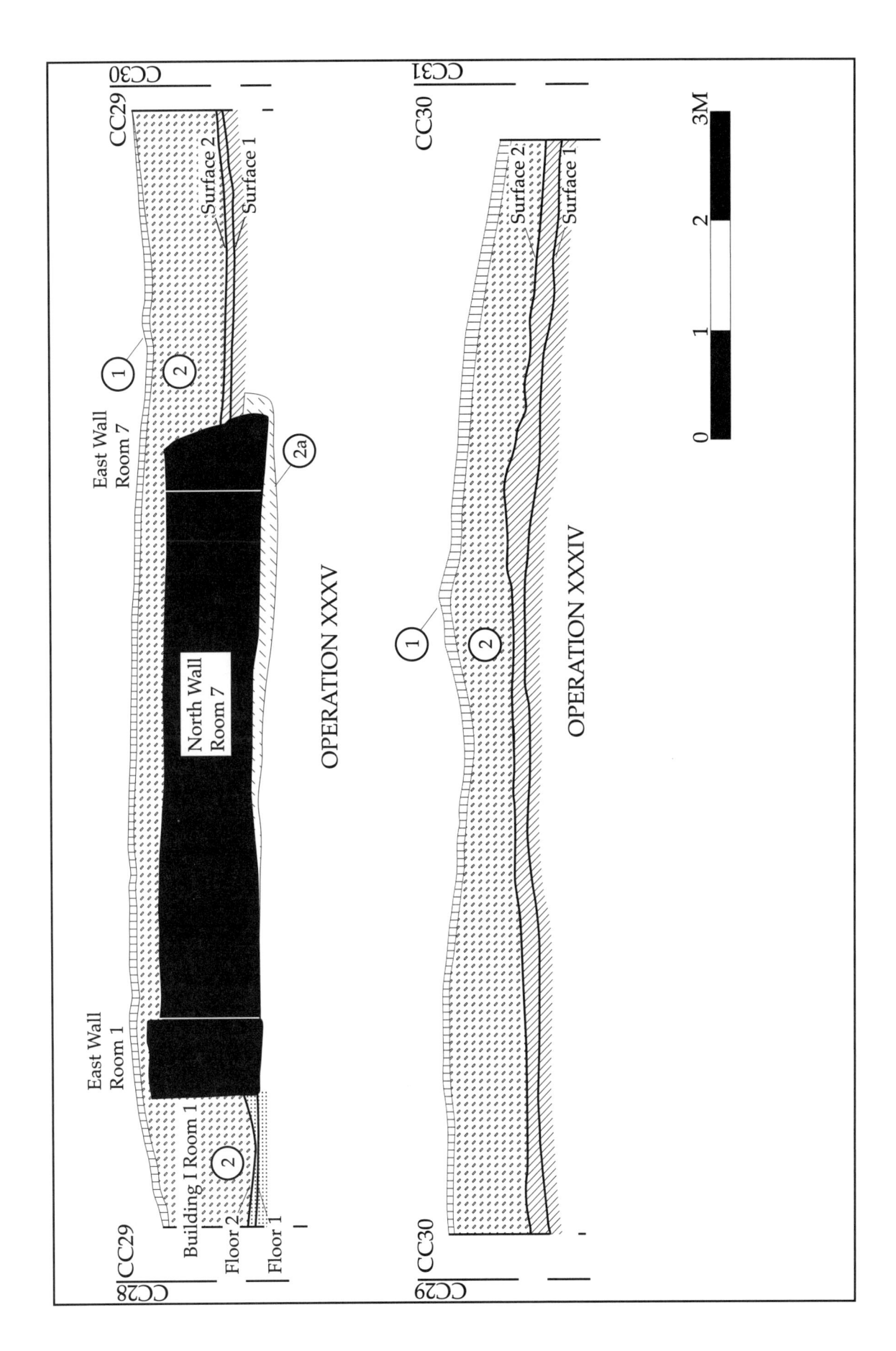

Figure 11. Hasanlu I: North section of Building I, Rooms 1 and 7 (CC29-CC30). See plan, Fig. 5.

FIGURE 12. HASANLU I: SMALL FINDS AND CERAMICS FROM BUILDING I

Fig. No.	Disposition	Field No.	Op	Grid	Location
1	TM	HAS 60-362	XXXV	CC29	Rm. 7, Str. 2
2	UPM 60-20-338		XXXIX	BB28	Str. 2
3	UPM 61-5-33	HAS 60-368	XXXV	CC29	Str. 2
4	UPM 61-5-918		XXXVI	CC28	Str. 1
5	UPM 60-20-331		XXXIX	BB28	Str. 2
6	UPM 61-5-917		XXXVI	CC28	Str. 1
7	UPM 60-20-329		XXXIX	BB28	Str. 2
8	UPM 61-5-920	HAS 60-1097	XXXV	CC29	Rm. 7, Str. 2

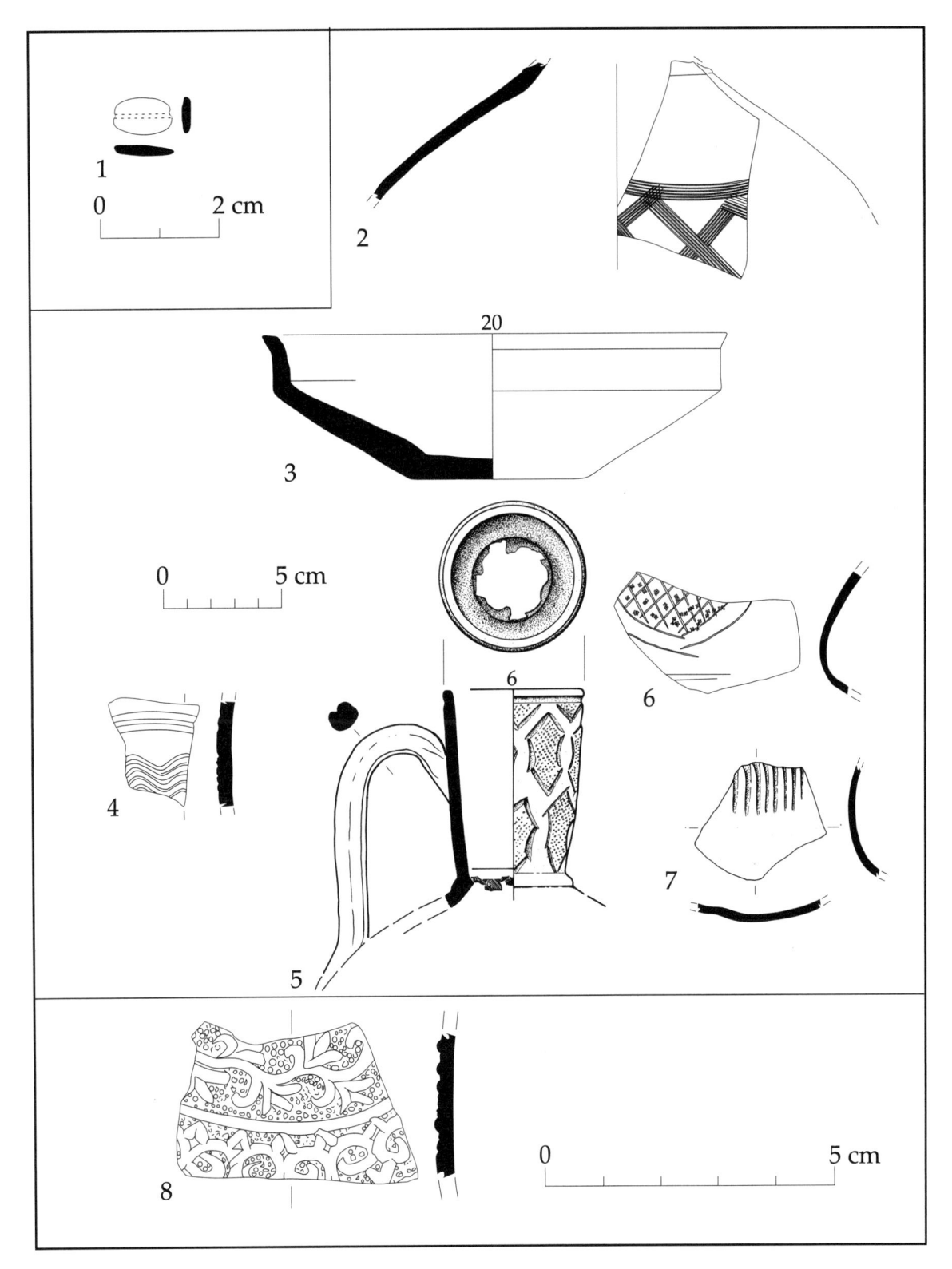

Figure 12. Hasanlu I: Small finds and ceramics from Building I.

eastern and western footings were brought in 50 cm. The mudbrick interior walls of the bin belonged to Phase 2 and measured 20 to 30 cm thick. The later exterior clay-paved Surface 2 (Figure 11) was associated with the Phase 2 structure and sealed the exposed portions of the Phase 1 stone footings of Building II. The walls of Building I Room 8 were founded on this surface. The excavators found no subsurface traces of a fortification wall to the east of Building II, although the fortification wall likely abutted it based on surface evidence such as soil discoloration and topography.

THE PERIOD I CERAMICS: GENERAL CHARACTERISTICS

The ceramic assemblage presented here represents nearly all the stratified Period I diagnostic material the expedition recorded and/or saved. In some instances, the excavators mention Period I ceramic diagnostics in the excavation notebooks, but these either were not saved or drawn, or were subsequently lost. Moreover, the excavators placed more emphasis on collecting the painted and glazed wares rather than on the plain wares. Therefore, the assemblage published here cannot be considered a fully representative sample. The majority of the ceramic sherds are currently stored in the collections of the Near East Section of the University of Pennsylvania Museum and the Metropolitan Museum of Art in New York.

Most of the Period I ceramics fit into four ware groups: red ware, buff ware, monochrome green-glazed ware, and overglaze painted ware. A few examples of underglaze painted and luster painted wares were also found.

Red ware is an unglazed earthenware and forms the bulk of the Period I ceramic assemblage. It ranges in color from Munsell 10R 5/6 red to 7.5YR 6/4 light brown. The majority of material falls between 2.5YR 5/4 reddish brown to 5/8 red, 5YR 5/4 to 5/6 reddish brown to yellowish brown, and 5YR 6/4 to 6/6 light reddish brown to reddish yellow. There is little appreciable difference between surface color and core color excepting the effects of weathering. Temper is generally fine-to-medium grit. In larger vessels, temper inclusions are larger. Most of the examples are evenly fired. Red ware was frequently decorated with comb incising.

The second category of unglazed earthenware, buff ware, ranges in color from 10YR 7/2 and 5Y 7/1 light gray to 10YR 7/3 very pale brown and 5Y 6/2 light olive gray. Exterior and interior colors are virtually identical, and little or no temper is visible. The ware is evenly fired. This ware tends to be decorated with elaborate incised and impressed decoration.

The paste of monochrome green-glazed ware is identical to that of the unglazed red ware. Most examples are 5YR 6/6 reddish yellow, 7.5YR 7/4 pink or 2.5YR 5/8 light red. The temper is fine-to-medium grit. The brilliant, clear, light green glaze is fairly consistent among the examples and was typically applied over a white slip. The exteriors of the vessels are often unglazed or haphazardly covered in glaze. Rims and bases tend to have thick applications of glaze. The ware is evenly fired and occasionally decorated in a simple *sgraffiato* pattern.

Overglaze painted ware consists of a fine stone paste body covered in a dark, cobalt blue glaze on the exterior and interior. This is, in turn, decorated with red and white paint (enamel) and gold leaf and refired in a muffle kiln.* At other sites, black was sometimes added to the palette used for painting relief tiles in this ware (Komaroff 2002:176). The technique for producing this ware, usually dubbed "lājvardīnah" ware after its cobalt blue or turquoise glaze, was described in the treatise of Abū'l-Qāsim of Kāshān in 1301 AD (Allan 1973).† Lājvardīnah ware gradually replaced the earlier mīnā'i painted tradition of the Saljūq period (Allan 1971:37; Grube 1976:254).

The Hasanlu overglaze painted ware assemblage includes small bowls/cups with T-shaped or "hammered" rims, larger bowls, plates, jars, bottles, jugs, and pitchers. Vessel walls are relatively thick, ranging from 0.4 to 0.9 cm. Other forms occurring in lājvardīnah ware but not attested at Hasanlu are thin-walled semi-globular bowls with simple, incurving rims, ewers, pear-shaped flasks, albarelli, sweet-meat dishes, mihrab-shaped tombstones, tile, and prayer

---

* See Wulff (1966:164–65, fig. 246) on the use of muffle kilns in traditional Persian ceramic production.
† On the naming of this ware and early attempts to date and locate its source of production see Ettinghausen (1936).

niches (Ettinghausen 1936:10). The turquoise glazed variety is absent at Hasanlu.

Typical design motifs on lājvardīnah ware are abstract or, more rarely, animals executed in gold with red painted outlines and details. Decorative motifs include vegetation, rosettes, peonies, lotus petals, circles, medallions with geometrical star designs, scrolls, wreaths, knots, imbricates, and dot-fringed escutcheons. Bowl interiors are often divided into trianguloid sections by a series of stripes radiating from the center. The sections are filled with intricate patterns following the triangular section and terminating in a tri-lobed pattern near the rim (Ettinghausen 1936:fig. 2). Animals and mythical beasts include fish, birds, simurghs, djeiran, phoenixes, Chinese dragons, nagas, and lion kylins. The interstices between the major design motifs are typically covered with tiny irregular scrolls, circles, and dots in white. Inscriptions almost never occur. The overall effect has been compared to "carved and bejewelled precious stones" (Mason 1997:18) and to the imitation of designs on luxury textiles imported from East Asia (Komaroff 2002:175 ff.). Under the Pax Mongolica of the later 13th and 14th centuries, the Chinese influence on the Iranian ceramic arts, already prevalent during the Saljūq period, greatly increased.[*] The ceramic assemblage from Hasanlu is no exception, although other elite eastern imports/imitations such as celadon appear to be missing.

Lājvardīnah ware vessels and tile may be attributed to a fairly short period of time spanning the late 13th and 14th centuries AD based on dated examples (715 AH/1315 AD and 776 AH/1374 AD) and literary and archaeological evidence (Pope 1938-39:1607; Allan 1971; Grube 1976:255-56; Carboni 2002:201-2).[†]

Period I Ceramics from Building I and the Surrounding Area (Figure 12, Color Plate A)

The small ceramic assemblage from Building I includes one red ware jar shoulder with horizontal and crisscrossing oblique, comb-incised bands (Figure 12:2). Plain buff ware includes a whole carinated bowl with a flat base (Figure 12:3). Examples of decorative techniques in buff ware are comb-incised wavy lines (Figure 12:4) and incised and impressed decoration (Figure 12:5, 6), including one pitcher with a strainer at the join between neck and shoulder and decorated with incised lozenges filled with impressed dots (Figure 12:5). Such decoration was also relatively common in disturbed deposits in the vicinity of Buildings I and II (e.g., Figure 27:6, 7). The other example has ovals filled with crosshatching, which in turn are filled with impressed rosettes (Figure 12:6). Figure 12:7 shows an irregularly shaped body sherd with a dimple and comb incising.[‡] Another sherd bears a molded design of bands filled with inter-linked arabesques and an undulating vine with spikey leaves (Figure 12:8).

---

[*] For a detailed discussion of innovations in ceramic production during the 13th century and the influence of the Mongols on northern Iran see Crowe (1987).

[†] The following are the dated examples and references to lājvardīnah ware:

1265-1281 AD—Takht-i Sulaimān, Summer Palace of Abaqa Khān. This site has evidence for the on-site manufacture of tiles. Lājvardīnah tiles were found at the site (Naumann and Naumann 1976).

1301 AD Abū'l-Qāsim Treatise. The author discusses the manufacture and popularity of lājvardīnah ware.

ca. 1307—Fragmentary hexagonal tile from Sulṭānīyeh (Luschey-Schmeisser 2000:381-382, pl. 5:3). The author also discusses a half-column in a peculiar variant of lājvardīnah (pl. 5:4) and a fairly well-known, but unprovenienced, lājvardīnah relief tile (398-404, pl. 13:1).

1308 AD—Letter from 'Alā' al-Dīn Muḥammad Shāh I, Sultan of Delhi (1295-1301 AD), to vizier Rashīd al-Dīn at Tabrīz. The sultan describes various Chinese export and lājvardīnah ware vessels he is sending to the vizier. The lājvardīnah ware is clearly not the product of China, but rather is being sent back to Persia as a diplomatic gift. See Lane (1957:7-8; Browne 1951:3:85, no. 47).

1315 AD—Star tile in the Collection of R. Ettinghausen, see Ettinghausen (1936:12, 1939:1691, no. 160).

1374 AD—J. W. Allan mentions this dated example of a cup, but does not cite a source (Allan 1971:37). He is referring to a cup in the Berlin Museum acquired in 1966 (cf. Soustiel 1985:98).

ca. 1385—Façade of "Ulugh Sultan Begum" Mausoleum in the Shāh-i Zinda complex of Samarqand (Golombek 1996:126; Golombek and Wilber 1988:no. 19, color pl. III, right).

[‡] For examples of vessels decorated with "dimpling" and incised and impressed decoration see Lane (1965:pl. 36:b) and Wilkinson (1973:301, 339, no. 25; 304, 341 no. 39). The Nishapur examples come from Tepe Madraseh and are "post-Samanid: a date of the eleventh century or later" (Wilkinson 1973:301). Wilkinson's no. 25 was found "at a high level in a site that was used into the twelfth century." The Hasanlu I example is certainly later in time and represents one of the many examples of the continuity between the plain and glazed earthenware assemblage of Period I and earlier, especially Saljūq, ceramic traditions.

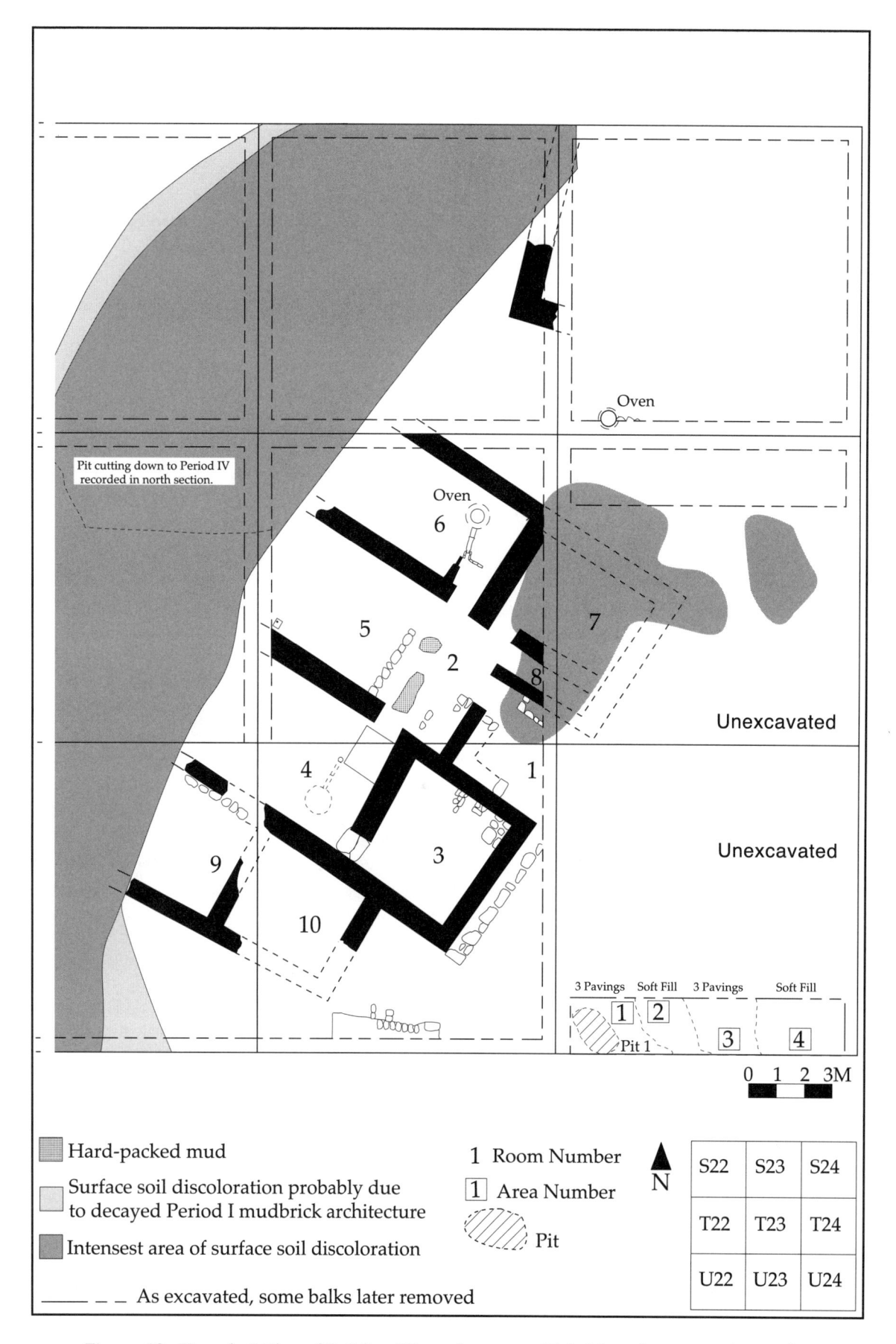

Figure 13. Hasanlu I: Plan of Building III, northwestern High Mound, excavated in 1962.

Monochrome green-glazed ware is restricted to a single coarse-bodied sherd with thick exterior glaze and a thin interior glaze on pinkish-buff fabric (Color Plate A:1). Overglaze painted ware designs include a medallion filled with an imbricate in gilt with red outlining (Color Plate A:2). Medallions are typically surrounded by a band of white lozenges and circles. Two other sherds, probably from the same vessel, have white lozenges, circles, and crescents/scrolls (Color Plate A:3, 4). Another example, probably part of a jug, has vertical gilt lines on the exterior (Color Plate A:5).

4

THE NORTHWEST HIGH MOUND

GRIDS Q25-26, R24-26, S22-24, T22-24, U22-24

On the highpoint of the northwest High Mound, the 1962 excavations revealed a large part of a house (Building III), associated outside spaces, and the corner of a second, badly eroded building in Grid S23 (Figure 13). The excavations in this area also cleared a long southwest-to-northeast running segment of the soil discoloration on the surface of the mound. The excavators found no subsurface indications of a fortification; however, the layout and construction of the adjacent domestic architecture (Buildings III and IV) provides strong evidence for dating this feature to Hasanlu I.

BUILDING III (FIGURE 13)

GRIDS T22-24, U22-24

Building III lay 20 to 25 cm below the surface and was oriented northeast to southwest. It seems Building III, missing a preserved northwestern wall, would have abutted the feature represented by the soil discoloration. This surface feature probably represents the remains of a wall completely made of *tauf* (see Building IV below). In support of this argument, the house's southeast-to-northwest-running walls are aligned perpendicular to the surface feature and run exactly up to the feature's eastern edge. In the area northwest of the feature, the excavators found a large pit of Period I (Figure 13, Grid T22), which had removed all archaeological remains down to Hasanlu Periods III and IV. The pit may have been a ditch running along the putative *tauf* fortification. Evidence for a Period I ditch was also found in Operation VII (J-K) (see below).

Building III is quite similar in layout and size to Building I on the southern High Mound (cf. Figures 5 and 13). It consists of a recessed entry area (Room 1) leading to a central court (Room 2) surrounded by five rooms (Rooms 3-7). Like Building I, this structure had rooms built against its outer wall with no preserved means of access (Rooms 9 and 10). The building was constructed of mudbricks measuring 22 x 22 x 4.5 cm with diagonal finger-impressed lines. The southwest wall of Rooms 3 and 4 incorporated a large number of small stones in its brickwork, and some of its bricks were baked. The southeast wall's exterior was lined with a stone and packed-mud bench 70 cm wide. On the southern end, the bench ended in a finely cut cornerstone. To the south of this building, excavations revealed plaster-surfaced open spaces in Grid U24 (Figure 13, Areas 1 and 3) associated with Period I ceramics and an oven in Grid U23 made of small stones and mud packing. A small circular oven was also found in the south balk of Grid S24.

Room 1 (3.57 x 4.20 m), the entry area, may have been completely open on its southeast side, but was probably enclosed like Building I Room 5. The western corner was lined with a stone bench (57 cm wide), the ends of which were formed by neatly cut cornerstones. As in Building I Room 5, a stone-lined

FIGURE 14. HASANLU I: SMALL FINDS FROM BUILDING III AND SURROUNDING AREA

Fig. No.	Disposition	Field No.	Material	Artifact Type and Description	Dimensions	Grid	Location
1	TM	HAS 62-9	Plaster	Wall decoration with lathe impressions	l. 11.9 cm, w. 4.3 cm, th. 2.7 cm	T23	Rm. 2, Str. 2
2	TM	HAS 62-17	Iron	Handle or ornament	l. 7.5 cm, w. 3.8 cm, th. 0.3 cm	U23	Rm. 3, Str. 3
3	Discarded	HAS 62-18	Iron	Nail	l. 3.2 cm, w. 0.7 cm, th. 0.3 cm	U23	Rm. 3, Str. 4
4	TM	HAS 62-2	Stone	Bluish-white bead	d. 1.7 cm, h. 0.5 cm	U23	Rm. 3, Str. 2
5	Discarded	HAS 62-4	Terracotta	Whorl	l. 2.4 cm, w. 2.4 cm, th. 1.8 cm	T23	Rm. 4, Str. 2
6	Discarded	HAS 62-19	Iron	Awl?	l. 4.7 cm, w. 0.9 cm, th. 0.4 cm	U23	Str. 3
7	Discarded	HAS 62-24	Iron	Unidentified	l. 2.8 cm	U23	Pit 3, Str. 2
8	Discarded	HAS 62-24	Iron	Unidentified	l. 3.8 cm	U23	Pit 3, Str. 2
9	TM	HAS 62-23	Carnelian	Bead	d. 1.1 cm, l. 0.8 cm	U23	Pit 3, Str. 2
10	UPM	HAS 62-22	Silver	Scale pan or measuring cup	l. 6.2 cm, w. 4.5 cm, th. 0.1 cm	U23	Rm. 4, Str. 2
11	UPM 63-5-26	HAS 62-21	Flint	Point	l. 5.4 cm, w. 1.7 cm, th. 0.7 cm	U23	Str. 2
12	UPM 63-5-2074		Glass	Plate	d. 12.0 cm, th. 0.3 cm	U23	Str. 2
13	Discarded	HAS 62-3	Iron	Ingot?	l. 5.0 cm, w. 2.1 cm, th. 1.1 cm	T23	Rm. 2, Str. 3
14	Discarded	HAS 62-8	Cu/Bronze	Coil ring	l. 2.3 cm, w. 2.0 cm, th. 0.6 cm	T23	Str. 2
15	UPM 63-5-236	HAS 62-1	Cu/Bronze	Pendant or weight	l. 3.6 cm, w. 1.3 cm	T23	Rm. 8, Str. 1
16	TM	HAS 62-6	Gr. Stone	Grinding stone	l. 6.8 cm, w. 6.8 cm, th. 5.4 cm	T23	Rm. 6, Str. 2
17	UPM 63-5-8	HAS 62-5	Gr. Stone	Burnisher	l. 12.5 cm, w. 9.8 cm, th. 3.2 cm	T23	Str. 2
18	Discarded	HAS 62-7	Terracotta	Whorl	l. 2.5 cm, w. 2.6 cm, th. 1.8 cm	T23	Str. 3

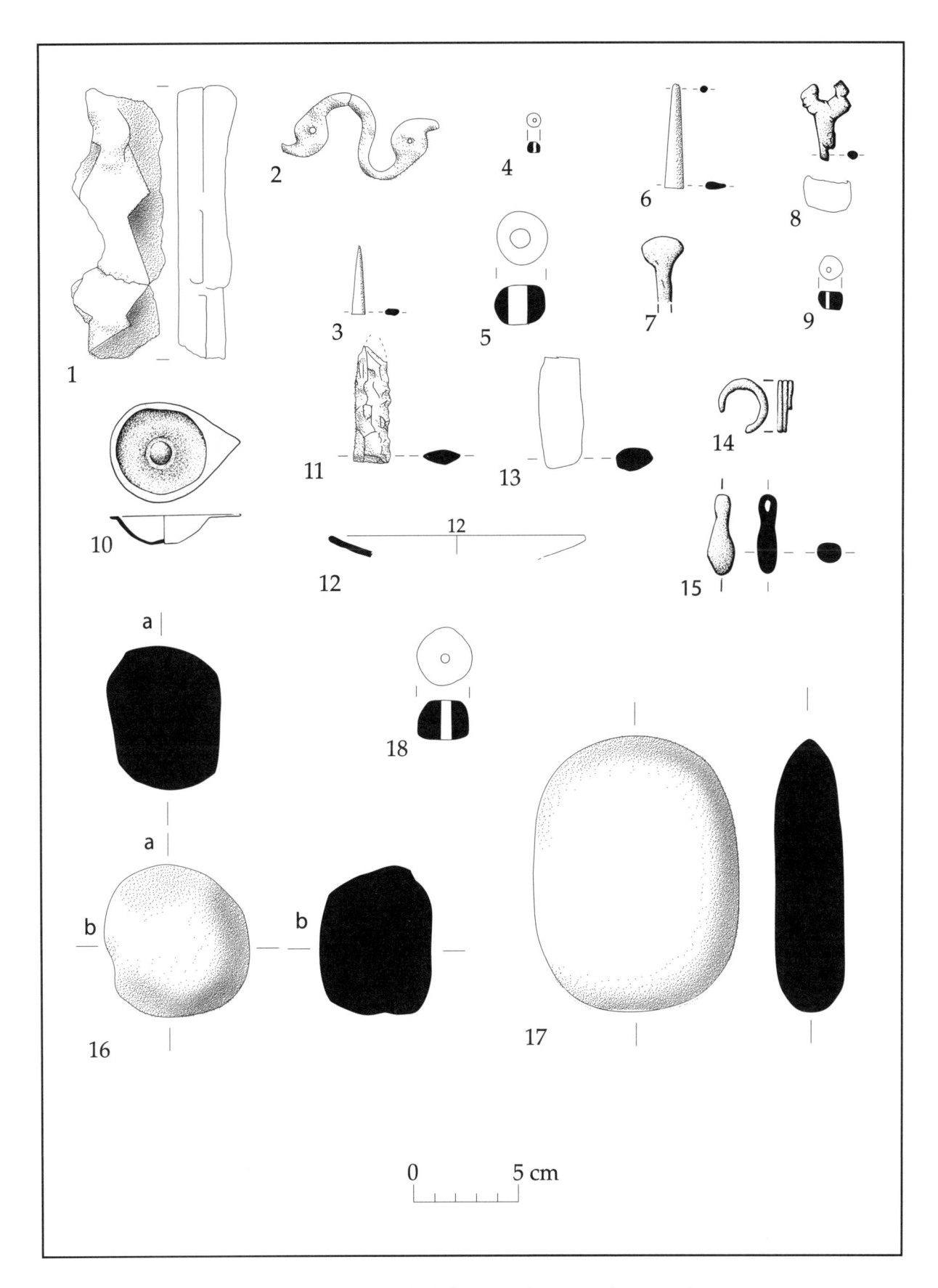

Figure 14. Hasanlu I: Small finds from Building III and surrounding area.

bin (interior space 30 cm wide) abutted one of the walls, in this case the northeast wall. In it the excavators found a fragmentary red ware jug (Figure 18:3) containing a single monochrome green-glazed body sherd (not saved). Below the final floor level (total number of floors unknown), the excavators found a line of large stones running parallel to the southwest wall and ending in the north at a point even with the southern face of the northwest wall. This footing, never mapped or drawn, may have been part of an earlier building phase in which a staircase, similar to Building III Room 8 (see below), was located on the southwest side of Room 1.

Room 2 (4.68 x 3.77 m), the central court, contained plaster fragments with impressions of wooden lattice 2 cm wide (Figure 14:1; Plate H), which likely originated from Room 4 (see below). At the northwest end of the court, the excavators found two areas of hard-packed mud, which they interpreted as the remains of benches or supports for posts. From this court, direct access was provided through doorways to Rooms 4-8.

Room 3 (4.36 x 4.02 m), situated in the southeast, had a floor of white plaster. A small stone bench (103 cm long x 61 cm wide) filled the room's northeast corner, and what the excavators interpreted as a stone-lined hearth abutted the northeast wall (Plate K). The excavators found no ash associated with this feature, but recovered an iron handle attachment and iron nails from the feature's fill (Figure 14:2-3; Plate K) and a bead on the room's floor (Figure 14:4). The doorway between Rooms 3 and 4 (width 95 cm) had a raised sill constructed of two flat stones covered in mud plaster.

Room 4 (4.60 x 5.80 m) contained a floor partially paved in flat stones coated in white plaster. On the floor, the excavators found fragments of white plaster decorated with concentric circles in low relief (HAS Sample 62-135) and a clay whorl (Figure 14:5). A rectangular plaster and stone basin (1.60 x 1.37 m), situated directly in front of the doorway to the court, was set below the surrounding floor level and served as a washbasin or toilet (Plates L and M). The stones were bonded with a thick white mortar. A drain hole lined with small stones and white plaster led to a drain constructed of clay pipe, terminating in a clay-lined pit with a baked clay rim. The segments measured 50 cm in length, 10 cm in diameter at the mouth, and 16 cm in diameter at the socket. An iron point (Figure 14:6) lay in the basin and two iron objects (Figure 14:7-8) and a light red carnelian bead (Figure 14:9) had fallen into the drainage pit. Just below the final floor paving, the excavators recovered a silver measuring cup or scale pan (Figure 14:10; Plate J), an iron fragment (discarded), a flint blade (Figure 14:11), and a rim sherd from a dark glass plate (Figure 14:12).

Room 5 (4.24 x 4.98 m) had a floor of white plaster. A stone footing running northeast to southwest and abutting the southwest wall probably represents a screen wall used to divide the space from the central court, a modification similar to that in Building I Rooms 1 and 2. In the room's southwestern corner, the excavators found a rectangular stone slab set into the floor. It measured 20 x 24 x 5 cm and had a circular depression in its top. This may have been the pivot stone for a door, which suggests there was a second door to Room 4 or that the putative architectural feature abutting the house to the northwest contained a passageway or interior space. An iron pig-ingot was the only small find from this room (Figure 14:13).

Room 6 (3.46 x 6.48 m), located to the north of the court, had a northeastern wall constructed of mudbrick on a stone footing one course high and five courses wide. The wall and footing were preserved 30 cm high. A short screen wall of baked brick and stone abutted the southwest wall. The final white plaster floor of the room sealed sherds of lājvardīnah ware, iridescent glass, and a bronze coil ring (Figure 14:14). A circular domed oven was set into the floor. The total height of the oven was 66 cm and the diameter at its base was 86 cm (Plates N and O). The oven had a flue constructed of two ceramic drainpipe segments. The segments and the construction technique are identical to the oven in Building I Room 4 (see above).

Rooms 7 and 8 to the northeast were only partially excavated. Room 8 (0.62 x 3.38 m) probably served as a stairwell leading to a second storey or the roof and contained sherds of lājvardīnah ware (Color Plates B:4 and C:1) and an iron pendant or weight sinker (Figure 14:15; Plate K).

The excavators recorded nothing of significance regarding Rooms 9 and 10 (4.12 x 3.80 m and 3.72 x 4.12 m, respectively), which adjoined the southeast wall. These rooms may have served a purpose similar to that of Building I Room 8, although there was no evidence in Operation U22 of a structure similar to Building II in Grid CC30.

BUILDING IV (FIGURE 15)

GRIDS Q25-26, R25-26

In this area, the excavators cleared a small exposure of two phases of a Period I house called Building IV(Figure 15). The building was oriented along, or formed part of, the putative fortification and lay 5 to 25 cm below the surface. The excavators found evidence of a circular bastion and an angle in the fortification wall almost exactly where Stein's 1936 sketch map predicts such features would be positioned.

The northwest wall, made of *tauf*, was 1.20 m wide. This wall, likely a segment of the fortification wall of the settlement, provides additional clues as to the origin of the surface soil discoloration and the missing northwest wall of Building III (see below).

The other walls of Building IV varied from 70 to 80 cm in width and were constructed of a combination of mudbricks measuring 21 x 21 x 7 cm and *tauf*, except for the second phase footing of the western wall of Rooms 1 and 4, which was constructed of stone. A semicircular foundation of a single course of large stones (average diameter 85 cm) abutted the north wall's exterior face. It is almost certainly the foundation of the circular bastion shown on Stein's sketch map positioned at the angle in the northwest fortification wall (Figure 3 Bastion No. 1). The bastion measured a total of 3 m in diameter, close to the size of Bastion 1 on Stein's map (Figure 3).

The excavators cleared two ovens and a Period I surface west of the building in Grid R25. They found few associated artifacts (Figure 16:1, 2). They also recovered ceramic diagnostics and small finds from a Period I surface in Grids S24 and S25 to the south (Figure 16:3, 4; 18:1, 6; 19:2); however, there were no other associated features or architectural remains there.

Room 1 (3.89 x 1.17 m) was probably entered through a doorway in the west end of the southeast wall, but the mudbrick of the southeast wall was too decayed to determine whether stones found there were footings or a raised sill (Figure 15). An adjoining stone paving along the southwest corner of the building favors reconstructing this feature as an entry. Three stone steps in the northwest corner of Room 1 led up to Room 2 to the northwest. Each riser stood only 5 cm high. The northeast wall of Room 1 has been reconstructed using the spatial extent and elevation of contemporary preserved floor levels in the area of Rooms 1 and 4. In Room 1, the area directly in front (southeast) of the stair had a hard-packed floor. To the east, this floor stopped along a line situated where we have reconstructed the western face of the room's northeast wall. Likewise, the floor of Room 4 stopped along a line equivalent to the eastern face of the reconstructed wall. As can be seen in the north section of R26 (Figure 17), the difference in floor levels between Rooms 1 and 4 was at least 50 cm. At some point during the building's use, the west wall of Rooms 1 and 2 was cut down and a new stone wall was built on top of it (Figure 17). Before the new stone wall was constructed, the earlier wall stub was cut by Pit 3. The excavators did not find a new floor level associated with the upper construction phase in Room 1. The only small find from this area, either from Room 1 or 4, was a frit bead (Figure 16:5).

Room 2 (3.96 x 3.78 m) had a clean brown mud floor, which lay 70 cm below the modern surface. Small finds were limited to a bluish-white glazed terracotta bead with incised herringbone decoration (Figure 16:6). This bead is almost certainly extrusive from Hasanlu Period IVB. A nearly identical bead was found *in situ* in Burned Building III Room 12 (HAS 62-548).

Room 3 (3.80 m north to south) contained an oven (diameter 60 cm) sunk into the floor. The floor lay 60 cm below the mound's surface. The south wall of Rooms 2 and 3 probably matched the angle of the building's north wall.

Room 4 (4.00 m north to south) contained a stone feature, possibly a bin, in the northwest corner of the excavated area.

The floors of Building IV sealed a deep pit (Pit 1, Strata 3b-3d) that cut down to Hasanlu Period IV levels (Figure 17). The pit is dateable to Hasanlu I based on the presence of lājvardīnah

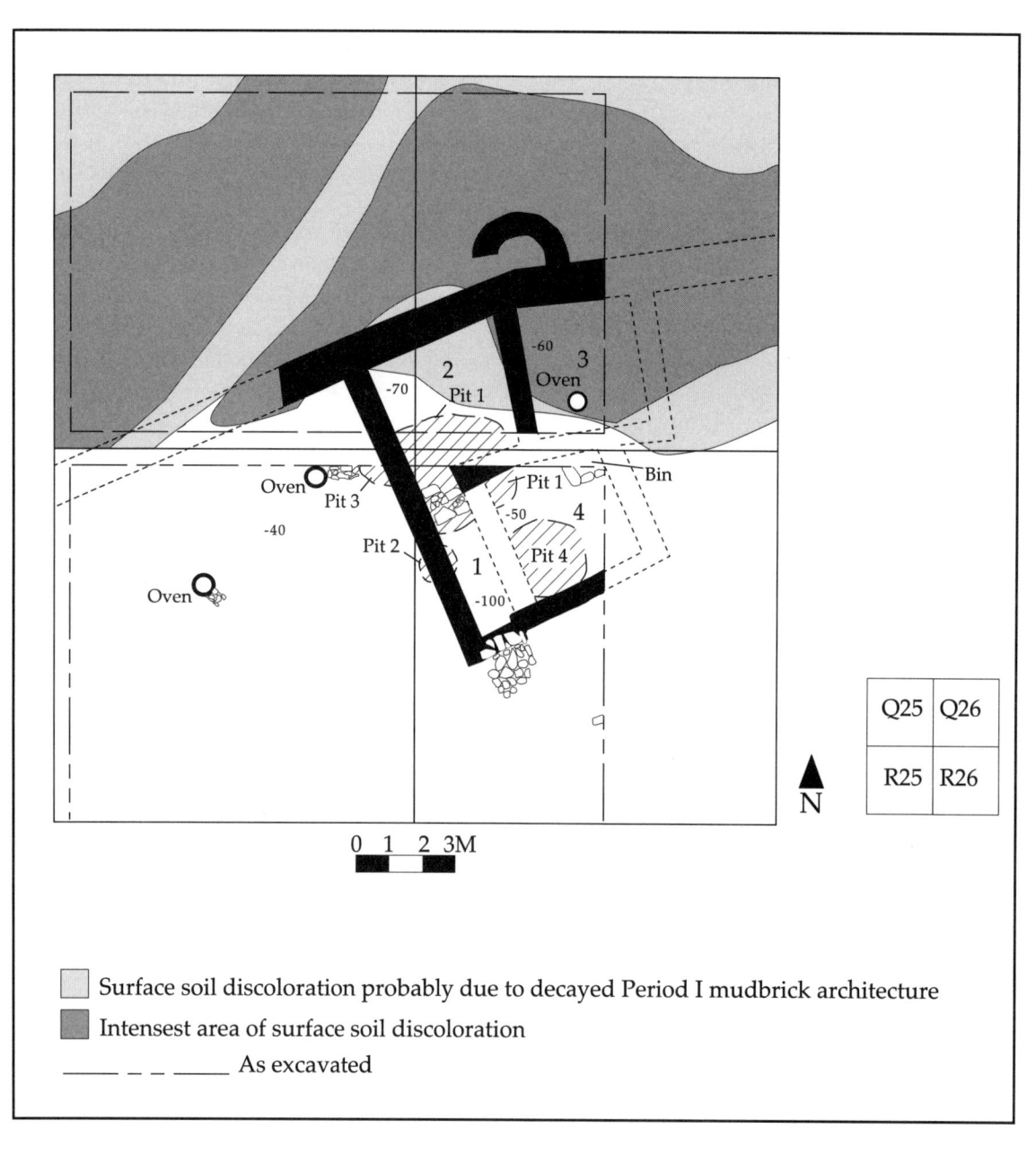

Figure 15. Hasanlu I: Plan of Building IV, the northern High Mound, excavated in 1962. See section Fig. 17.

ware (Color Plate D:6) and glass with enamel decoration in red and blue (Figure 16:7) found at the pit's bottom—a decorative technique common to this period. Glass painted in copper luster (Figure 16:8) and a cylindrical frit bead (Figure 16:9) were also found in the pit. Overall the pit matrix was similar to the surrounding soil, but the excavators easily distinguished the cut since the fill contained numerous white flecks, especially near the bottom. The building's Phase 1 west wall and floor also sealed a small Period I pit (Pit 2) containing a sherd of lājvardīnah ware (Figure 15). Another pit below the building, Pit 4, contained a sherd of Sulṭānābād ware (Color Plate E:2).

THE FORTIFICATION WALL

The best evidence for the design and construction of the Ilkhanid fortification wall was discovered in this excavation area. As indicated by the northwest wall of Building III, segments of *tauf* wall were likely used to enclose the Period I settlement, which would have been easier and cheaper to produce than a wall built completely of mudbrick or baked mudbrick. Moreover, such a circumvallation would have deteriorated faster than mudbrick walls after the abandonment of the settlement and would have been more difficult for the excavators to find when poorly preserved, which would explain the missing northwest wall of Building III.

Evidence favoring the existence of a settlement wall largely built of *tauf* segments includes:

(1) The Building IV wall follows the surface soil discoloration and the line of the fortification wall on Stein's sketch map,
(2) The wall's construction technique, size, and alignment are different from the rest of Building IV's walls,
(3) The wall is the same thickness as other putative segments of the Period I circumvallation—i.e., the *tauf* south wall of Building I Room 8 and the south stone footing of Phase 1 of Building II.

However, the potential fortification wall found in the Operation IX trench does not fit this pattern, being much wider and constructed of square mudbricks (see Figure 5, Grid BB28). Moreover, a wall (Wall B) found in Operation VII J-K below the surface soil discoloration is narrower and built of mudbrick (Figure 20, see below), but, it probably formed part of a domestic structure that sat astride the fortification wall similar to Building I.

PERIOD I CERAMICS FROM BUILDING III AND THE SURROUNDING AREA (FIGURE 18, COLOR PLATES A–C)

Red ware forms from Building III include a bottleneck or spout with an incised groove below the rim, probably for attaching a string for securing a stopper (Figure 18:1) and two comb-incised jugs (Figure 18:2, 3). Such jugs were quite common in red ware on the High Mound. Figure 27:3 and 4 show two other types. Buff ware ceramics include incised registers of cross-hatching filled with impressed rows of circles (Figure 18:4), impressed decoration on the neck of a pitcher (Figure 18:5), and an incised knob-ended spout or the handle to a lid (Figure 18:6). Two examples that do not fit the unglazed ware categories are a tan sherd painted in dark brown (Figure 18:7) and a dark red and black cooking pot with impressed decoration (Figure 18:8). Cooking pots were probably fairly common in the Hasanlu I assemblage but were unlikely to have been saved during the excavations. This example is fairly typical of medieval cooking pot forms (Redford 1998:fig. 3.12:D). The excavators also noted the presence of jug sherds with wavy-line combed incising (not collected).

Monochrome green-glazed ware is restricted to a large flaring-sided bowl with a heavy glaze at the rim, giving it a much darker appearance (Color Plate A:6). The glaze and white slip were haphazardly applied to the upper portion of the vessel's exterior.

The excavators found several sherds of overglaze painted ware in this area. Two rims from small lājvardīnah jars, possibly from the same vessel, are decorated with gild lozenges outlined in red and white enamels (Color Plate B:1, 2). The overglaze white paint has worn off the sherd shown in Color Plate B:1. A flat base has an unglazed exterior and bears a flower-petal design in reserve blue glaze, red

FIGURE 16. HASANLU I: SMALL FINDS FROM BUILDING IV AND SURROUNDING AREA

Fig. No.	Disposition	Field No.	Material	Artifact Type and Description	Dimensions	Grid	Location
1	UPM 63-5-2073	HAS 62-608	Alabaster	Translucent bowl fragment	d. 16 cm	R25	Str. 2
2	Discarded	HAS 62-609	Glass	Purple iridescent bead	d. 1.0 cm, th. 0.9 cm	R25	Str. 2
3	TM	HAS 62-671	Bone	Arrowhead	7.9 cm, shaft d. 0.4 cm	S25	Str. 2
4	UPM 63-5-2	HAS 62-670	Stone	Gray tankard	d. 13 cm, h. 12.5 cm	S25	Str. 2
5	Discarded	HAS 62-623	Frit	Bead	d. 1.5 cm, l. 1.8 cm	R26	Str. 1/2
6	UPM 63-5-293	HAS 62-607	Terracotta	Blue-glazed bead	d. 1.3 cm, l. 5.1 cm	Q26	Str. 1
7	UPM 63-5-2075	HAS S62-99	Glass	Blue and red painted sherd	th. 0.25 cm	Q26	Dump
8	UPM 63-5-2050		Glass	Luster-painted glass rim sherd	th. 0.25 cm	T23	Rm. 2, Str. 2
9	UPM 63-5-2076	HAS S62-98	Frit	Brown bead	d. 1.25 cm, l. 3.5 cm	R26	Pit 1, Str. 3

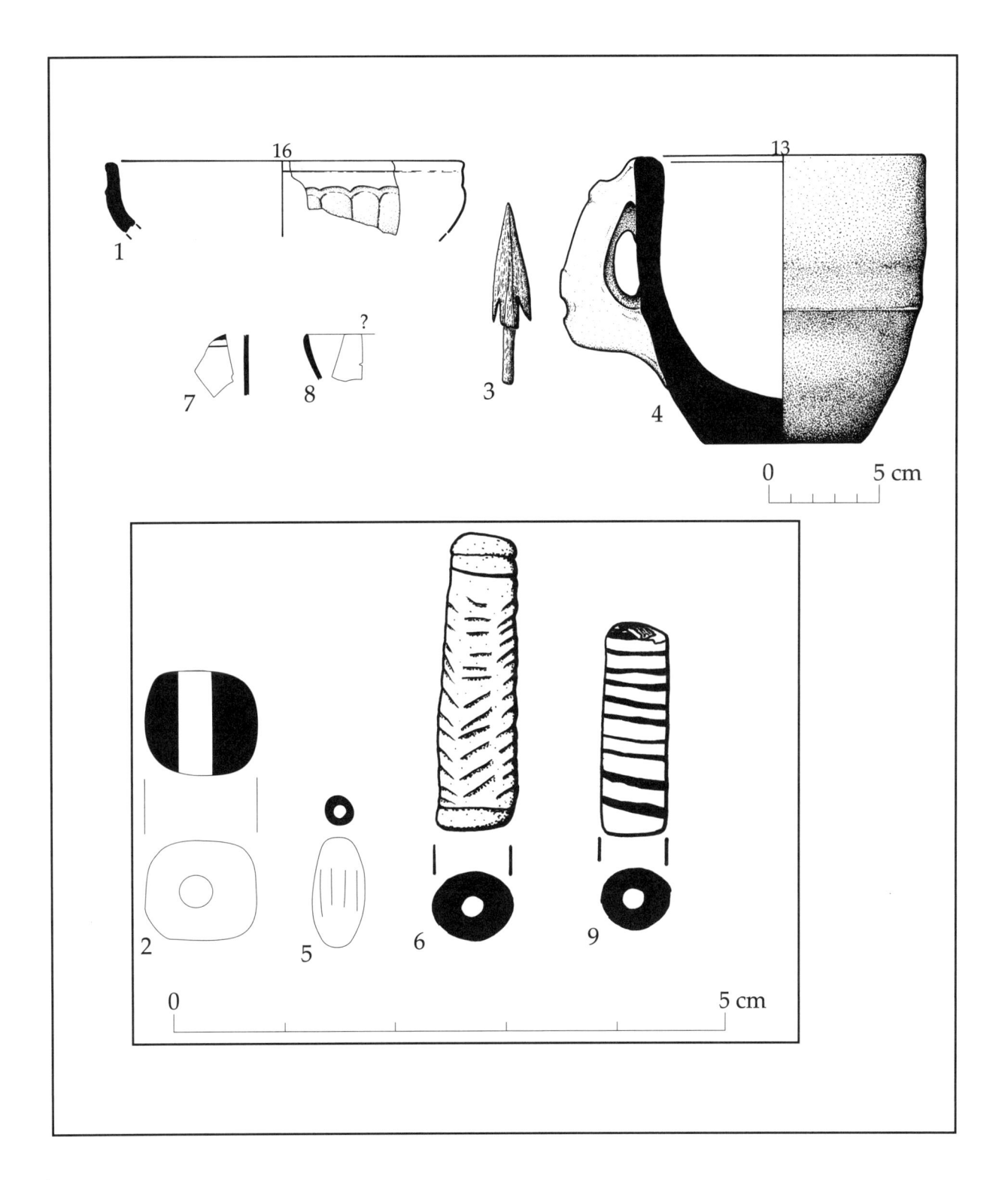

Figure 16. Hasanlu I: Small finds from Building IV and surrounding area.

paint, and gild on its interior (Color Plate B:3). Two plates or shallow bowls are decorated on their exterior in white-painted vertical lines (Color Plate B:4, 5). One from Building IV has a diamond-shaped medallion filled with an imbricate painted in red outline filled with gilding (Color Plate B:4). The other has what are likely a pair of water fowl amid vegetation executed in red paint and gilt fill surrounded by eroded white scrolls and dots (Color Plate B:5).*

The larger part of a lājvardīnah jar came from Building III Room 8 (Color Plate C:1; Plate P). This is the best-preserved lājvardīnah vessel from Hasanlu and provides fairly complete examples of the design motifs shown on other smaller fragments from the site. This case shows a repeating pattern with large circular medallions filled with imbricates and flanked by leafy branches. Two bands of horizontal lines and repeating lozenges, crescents, and dots frame this design. The interior is decorated with at least two more rows of lozenges, crescents, and dots, one on the interior of the rim and the other deep inside the vessel's interior, where it was surely difficult to paint (as the crooked line of the motif confirms). The exterior design is fairly typical of lājvardīnah vessels (cf. Pinder-Wilson 1969:43, no. 140). The gilt lines outlined in red paint underscoring the lozenge band below the rim exterior, above the lowest lozenge band on the body and surrounding the medallion, have direct parallels on Iranian metalwork of the 13th and early 14th centuries (see for example Rossabi 2002:18, fig. 12; Melville 2002:47, fig. 44) and as a framing device in manuscripts (Melville 2002:220, fig. 269). Another glazed ware attested in this area was a body sherd painted in black under a clear blue glaze (Color Plate C:2). This "horseshoe and dot" motif also occurs on luster ware from the site (Color Plate F:2).

Period I Ceramics from Building IV and the Surrounding Area (Figure 19; Color Plates D, E)

From Building IV and its surrounding area the excavators collected red ware jars with bands of comb-incised decoration (Figure 19:1, 2)[†] and a high-necked jar with five incised lines on its neck (Figure 19:3). Incised designs on closed vessels with handles also include an abstract vine motif (Figure 19:4). Open forms include a large vat with ledged rim (Figure 19:5) and a small bowl with flat base and rounded rim (Figure 19:6). Few large vessels, such as vats, storage jars, and bowls, appear to have been saved by the excavators and may have occurred in higher frequency than reflected by the recorded assemblage. Larger forms were produced almost exclusively in red ware, such as a large bowl and jar with incised design collected from the site's surface (Figure 27:1, 2). A flat base probably comes from a pitcher or jug (Figure 19:7).

Buff ware examples include a jar or pitcher rim with the remains of a strainer just below the rim (Figure 19:8) and a comb-incised pitcher or ewer (Figure 19:9).

Monochrome green-glazed ware examples include a bowl decorated in the *sgraffiato* technique over a white slip (Color Plate D:1) and another with the green glaze applied over a white-slipped interior (Color Plate D:2). The glaze appears much darker on the unslipped exterior portions. The excavators also found a button base in this ware (Color Plate D:3). The bowl shown in Color Plate D:1 with simple *sgraffiato* under colored glaze is nearly identical to an example from Haraba-Gilan (Aslanov, Ibragimov, and Kaşkaj 1997:420, pl. 10, lower left) and is similar in glaze color, paste, and incised designs to an example of "Iranian *Sgraffiato*" in the Tareq Rajab Museum attributed to 12th century Iran (Féhérvári 2000:84, no. 84). Féhérvári dates this ware to the 12th and 13th centuries and a brief period after the Mongol invasion (Féhérvári 2000:85). Similar monochrome green-glazed ware has also been found in the excavations at Takht-i Sulaimān, so-called Garrus Ware (see esp. Naumann and Naumann 1976; Schnyder 1972), and in neighboring regions (Allan 1974). The consensus on the dating of this ware, and closely related slip-carved types, is they belong to the 11th to late 13th centuries (*contra* Grube 1976:110, n. 1). Based on sealed deposits from Hasanlu Period I, we can state that such green-glazed *sgraffiato* ceramics

---

* For a similar design element in lājvardīnah ware see Pope (1938:V:pl. 751B).
[†] This technique was also used in Period VI, the first half of the 2nd millennium BC, a fact that led to much misidentification of surface material until it was documented by excavation.

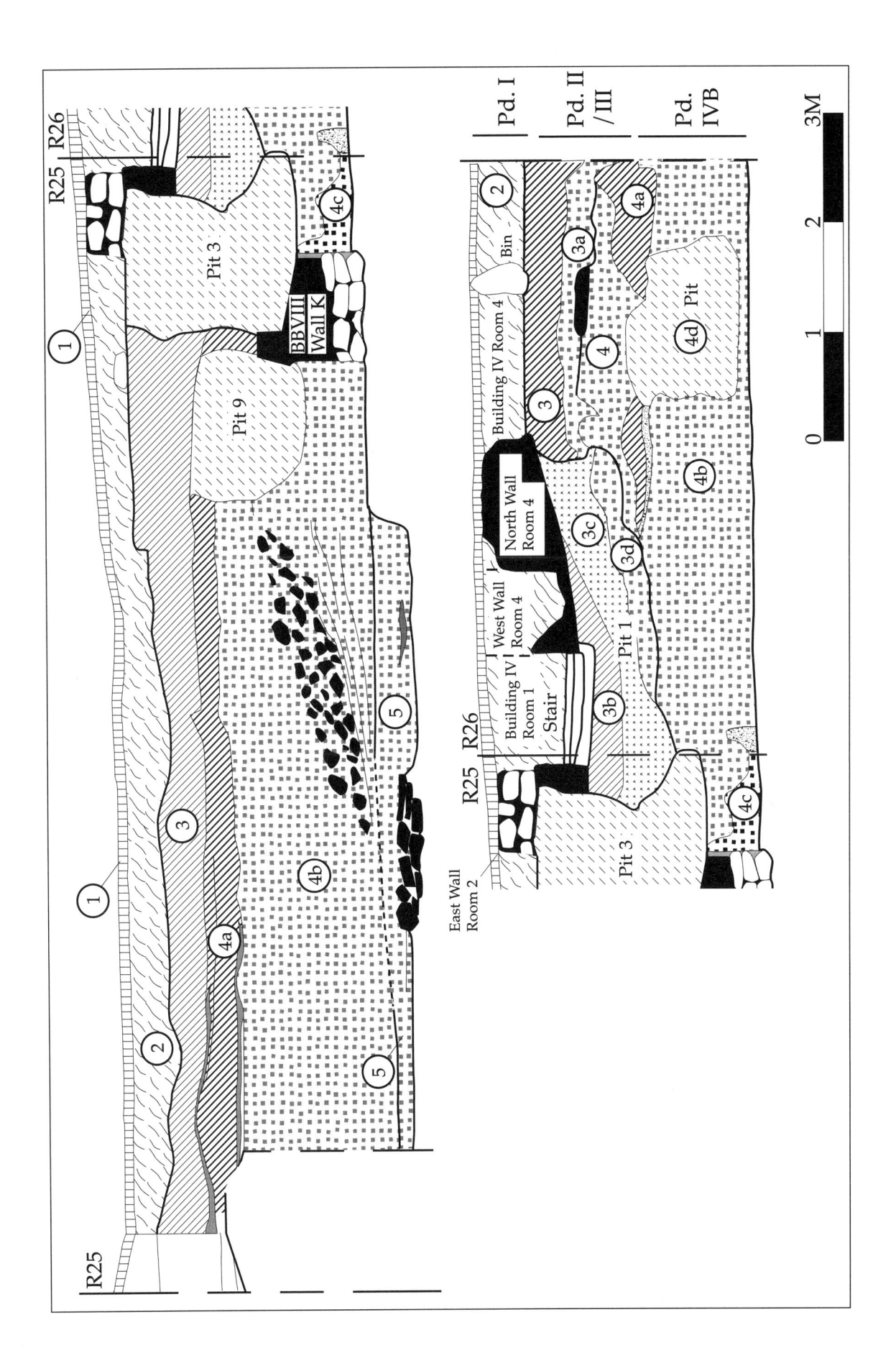

Figure 17. Hasanlu I: North section of Building IV (R25-R26). See plan, Fig. 15.

FIGURE 18. HASANLU I: CERAMICS FROM BUILDING III AND SURROUNDING AREA

Fig. No.	Disposition	Field No.	Grid	Location
1	UPM 63-5-2053		S24	Str. 2
2	UPM 63-5-2054		T23	Str. 2/3
3	Discarded	HAS 62-823	T23	Rm. 1, Str. 2
4	UPM 63-5-2050		T23	Rm. 2, Str. 2
5	UPM 63-5-2068		U23	Str. 3
6	UPM 63-5-2052		S24	Str. 1
7	UPM 63-5-2061		T23	Rm. 2, Str. 2
8	UPM 63-5-2055		T23	Str. 1

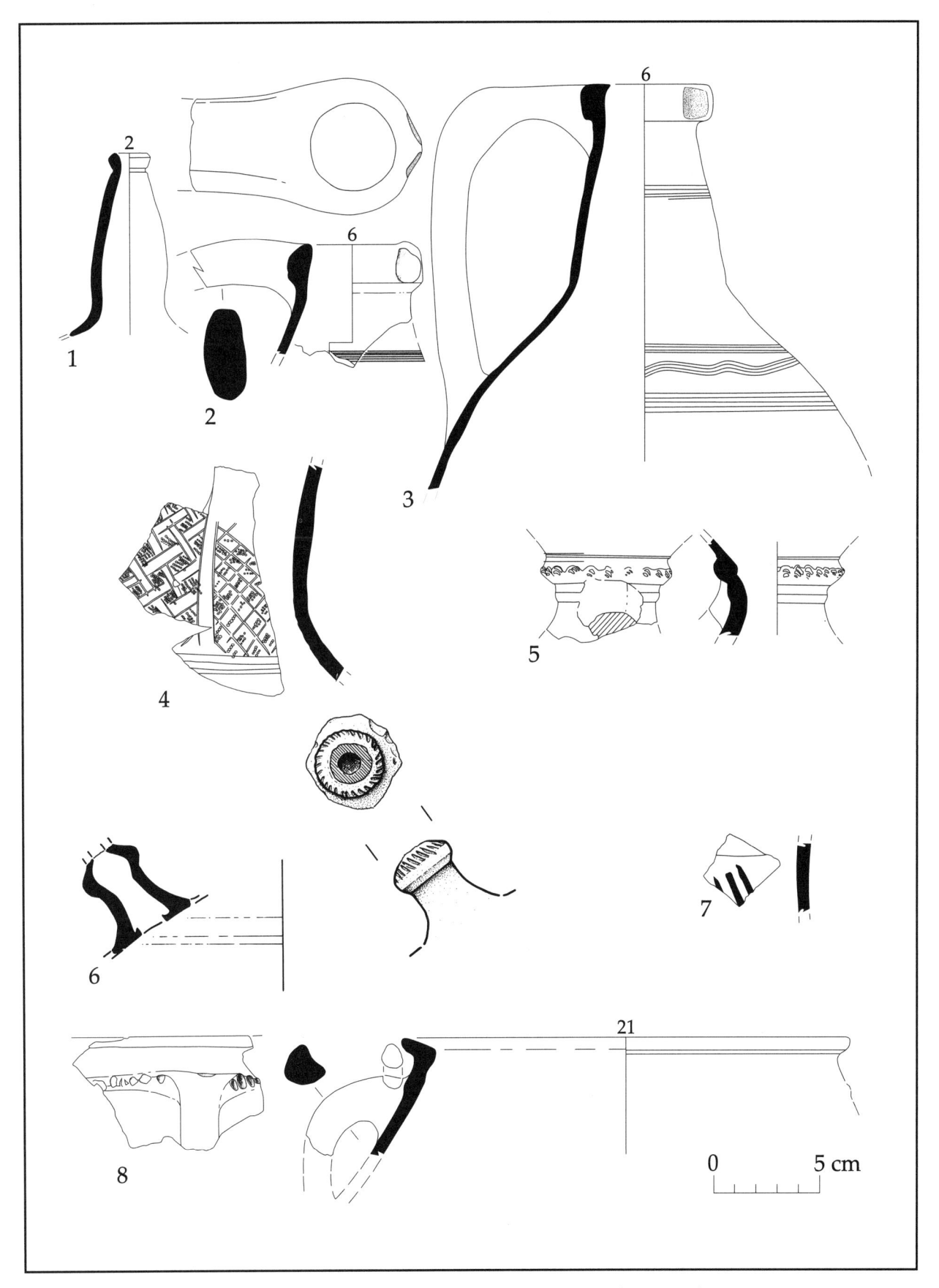

Figure 18. Hasanlu I: Ceramics from Building III and surrounding area.

Figure 19. Hasanlu I: Ceramics from Building IV and Surrounding Area

Fig. No.	Disposition	Field No.	Grid	Location
1	UPM 63-5-2071		Q26	Str. 1
2	UPM 63-5-2066		S25	Str. 2
3	UPM 63-5-2069		R26	Str. 2
4	UPM 63-5-2065		R26	Str. 2
5	UPM 63-5-2056		Q26	Str. 2
6	UPM 63-5-2072		R26	Str. 2
7	UPM 63-5-2070		S25	
8	UPM 63-5-2063		S25	Str. 2
9	UPM 63-5-2067		R26	Str. 2

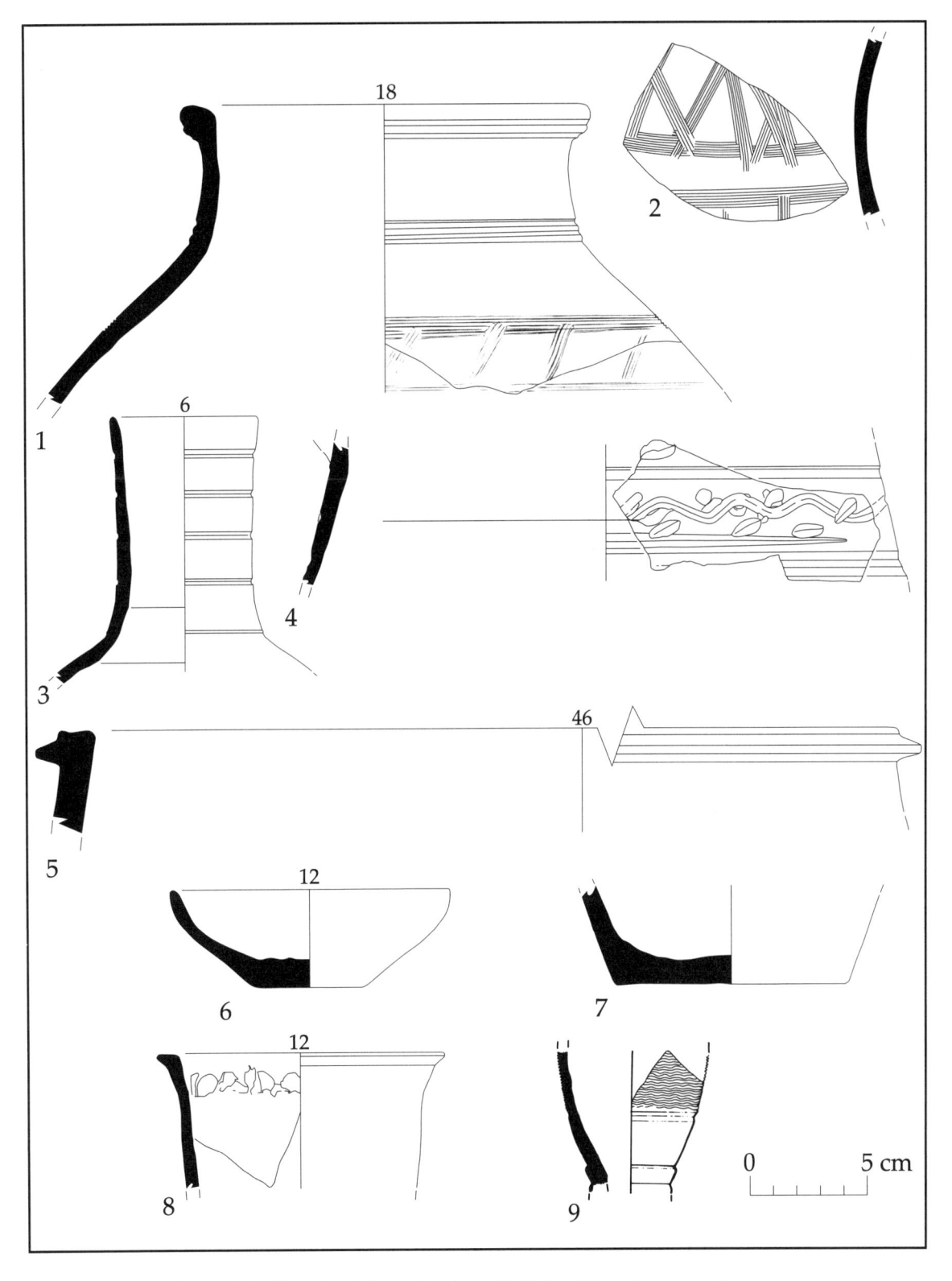

Figure 19. Hasanlu I: Ceramics from Building IV and surrounding area.

were contemporary to overglaze painted lājvardīnah ware, and their date range should therefore be extended to include at least the early Ilkhanid Period (cf. McNicoll 1983:64).

Overglaze painted ware was found in Pit 1, sealed by Building IV (see above), including a bottleneck (Color Plate D:6) with deteriorated overglaze painting of bands of lozenges and a body sherd decorated with the standard vegetal motif used to flank medallions (Color Plate D:7). Lājvardīnah ware was also found on the floors of Building IV (Color Plate D:4, 5). In Grid S25, the excavators recovered two lājvardīnah sherds in the upper strata with a circular medallion filled with an imbricate in gilt outlined in red paint (Color Plate D:8, 9). Gilt lozenges outlined in red and a band of white crescents and dots surround the medallion.

The excavators recovered other types of fine glazed wares in this area. One small luster ware sherd of copper color comes from the S25 surface (Color Plate E:1). Another luster ware sherd of identical color scheme and fabric was found on the surface of the mound (Color Plate F:2). This bowl form with "hammered" or overhanging rim is decorated on the exterior with a stylized Kufic inscription and a row of "horseshoes and dots/circles" on the rim. It is of the so-called Kāshān style and has been dated to the earlier 13th century (cf. Watson 1985: 108-109, fig. 87). The discovery of these luster ware sherds with other fine wares attributable to the Ilkhanid period lends support to Grube's assertion (1976:261) that such luster wares likely survived into the middle of the 14th century. A single sherd with stone paste fabric and interior underglaze painting in black, blue, green, and gray on an opaque white ground, so-called Sulṭānābād ware (Grube 1976:261-268), comes from R26 Pit 4 (Color Plate E:2). The exterior surface was too deteriorated for any assessment. A bowl with a nearly identical interior design resides in the Kestner Museum, Hanover (Weiers 1989:pl. 44). The reconstructed design of the Hasanlu bowl sherd is typical of so-called Sulṭānābād ware and is quite similar to the repertoire of painted designs on lājvardīnah ware. This similarity led Ettinghausen to date lājvardīnah ware to the same period as Sulṭānābād ware and to postulate that it was manufactured at the same production centers (Ettinghausen 1936:10 ff.).

One fragmentary bowl with stone paste fabric and a hammered rim was painted in black under clear blue glaze (Color Plate E:3). Sherds from this vessel were found in Grid R26 Pit 1 and on the Period 1 surface of Grid S25. The exterior was decorated in a register of birds separated by abstract vegetal motifs. The rim bears a row of fish, a motif on vessels often attributed to the 12th and 13th centuries of the Kāshān style on similar underglaze painted wares (Lane 1953:45-46, figs. 86 and 91; Grube 1976:189, no. 136). The interior has panels of vegetation alternating with fields of parallel rows of horizontal zigzags. An almost identical example in the Teheran Museum comes from Takht-i Sulaiman and purportedly dates to the 14th century AD (Kiani 1978:63, no. 115). This style is usually referred to as the "International" or "Panel" style; it is typical of underglaze painted ware of the 14th Century (Mason, Bailey, and Golombek 1996:111) and is related to Sulṭānābād ware (Lane 1957:10-13; Soustiel 1985:198-99).

5

THE NORTHERN STRATIGRAPHIC TRENCH

OPERATIONS I AND VII (FIGURES 20-22)
GRIDS N28-T28

In an effort to section the upper levels of the entire High Mound, a long, north-south stratigraphic trench was laid out bisecting the mound's central depression. This trench, comprised of Operations I, II, and VII on the north end of the High Mound and Operations IX and XIV on the south, was excavated between 1956 and 1958 (Figure 4). Operation VII was divided into four long segments labeled, from north to south, B-F, G-H, J-K, and L-M and separated by balks. Segments J-K (1.7 x 25.6 m) and L-M (1.7 x 13.6 m) revealed architectural remains that probably date to Hasanlu Period I. Two stone-paved stairways in Operation I (9.0 x 7.0 m) likely date to Period I. Few finds were recorded from these operations.

In Operation VII J-K, excavation revealed a short segment of a wall (Wall B) in the area of the putative Period I fortification as mapped using the surface soil discoloration (Figures 21 and 22, Strata 2, 3, and 5). Moreover, Wall B corresponds closely, that is within a few meters, to the point at which the inner circumvallation in Stein's 1936 sketch map would intersect the trench. Wall B (width 80 cm) was founded on Stratum 4, a hard layer of burned bricky material, and sealed by Stratum 2 (loose powdery wash) (Figure 21). Surfaces 1 and 2, separated by a layer of hard bricky fill (Stratum 3), were associated with this wall. The continuation of these surfaces to the south in Grid Q28 was not recorded, and thus their exact extent remains indefinite. The presence of two building phases is similar to the construction histories of Period I Buildings I-V. A circular oven was set on Surface 2 and is similar to other above-ground Period I ovens in terms of size (diameter 60 cm) and construction.

North of Wall B the excavators found evidence for a shallow ditch (depth 90 cm), possibly a defensive feature. This cut was filled with a pebbly matrix (Stratum 5), which was in turn partially covered by a layer of stones. Subsequent to the construction of Wall B a sloping fill of unspecified composition accumulated against its north face and atop the layer of stones.

Strata 1-3 and the associated architecture likely date to Period I based on the total depth of the Strata 1-3 deposit below the mound's surface, Wall B's orientation, size, and alignment with the surface soil discoloration; and, the oven's similarity to others found in secure Period I contexts.

The only diagnostic sherd recorded for Operation VII J-K, a rim sherd from a Classic Triangle Ware bowl found in Stratum 3 (illustrated in Dyson 1999:fig. 1:g), dates to Period IIIA (400-280 BC) and may be in a secondary context. During the excavations, Dyson recorded the following observations on Operation VII, "This trench cut through the final occupation of the mound, a mediaeval Islamic fortification [Wall B] linked with the two stone stairways reported previously. The Islamic stratum is about sixty centimeters deep [in the south end of the trench] and yields lime-encrusted sherds of heavy, plain-ware [i.e., red ware and buff ware] water jugs

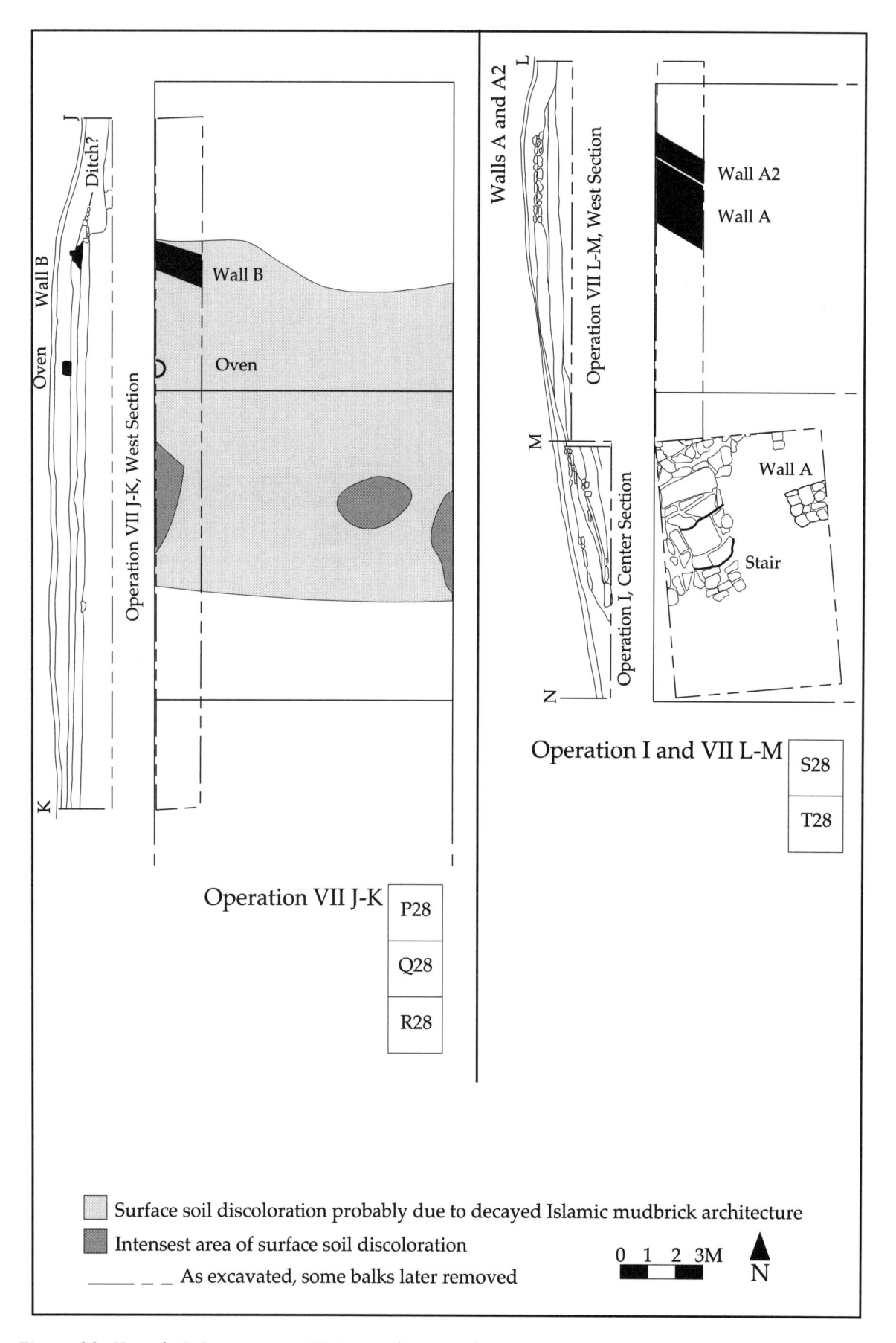

Figure 20. Hasanlu I: Operations I, VII L-M, and VII J-K, the northern High Mound. See also Figs. 21 and 22.

with flat bases and almost vertical sides" (1958b:32). Islamic ceramics with gray-buff cores, rope designs, and flat bases are also mentioned as having been found in this area.

Two stone footings in Operation VII L-M, Walls A and A2, probably date to Period I. Wall A was founded on a layer of hard bricky fill (Stratum 4), which was cut away to the north and south of the wall (Figure 22). Stratum 4 is almost certainly equivalent to Stratum 3 of Operation VII J-K, and so Wall A would be contemporary to the oven attributed to Period I there and the latter use-phase of Wall B. Wall A2, which abuts and runs parallel to Wall A, postdates the cutting of Stratum 4 on the north side of Wall A, and is therefore slightly later. Like the Period I architecture in Operation VII J-K, Walls A and A2, and the mudbrick collapse of Wall A (Stratum 3), were sealed by a layer of loose, powdery wash (Stratum 2). The fact that Walls A and A2 ran parallel to Wall B in Operation VII J-K lends additional support for dating them to Period I. No Period I finds were recorded for this trench.

A narrow balk separated Operation VII L-M from the north end of Operation I (Figure 20). The only Period I diagnostic materials in Operation I were unstratified sherds near the surface that were not recorded. Two phases of a stone-paved stairway were found in this area, an initial construction and a later rebuilding. The stairways are difficult to date with certainty since their stratigraphic relationship to architecture in adjacent Operation VII L-M is unclear due to the cutting of Operation VII Stratum 4 in Period I (Figure 22) and the existence of a balk between Operations I and VII L-M that was only partially removed during excavation (Figure 20). The fact that there were two construction phases of the same architectural feature hints at a Period I date for the stairways, which in previous reports have been attributed to both Periods I and IIIB (Dyson 1956:284; 1957:38). The stone footings of Operation I Wall A, preserved one course high and 1.37 m wide, were contemporary to the final phase of the stairs.

The architectural remains from Operation VII J-K likely represent the remains of another Period I house located along, or forming part of, the Ilkhanid circumvallation. Walls A and A2 in Operation VII L-M are more puzzling. The thickness of Wall A suggests that something other than a residential structure existed at the center of the High Mound near the central depression. This wall was either widened at a later date or was abutted by another later building (Wall A2). Given the limited exposure, any interpretation is highly conjectural, but these walls may have formed part of a structure associated with the stone-paved stairways and the wall footing found in Operation I. The presence of a large, important structure in this area would follow the Mongol custom in city planning of locating important buildings "at the city center or the center of its northern area, facing south" (Masuya 1997:212).

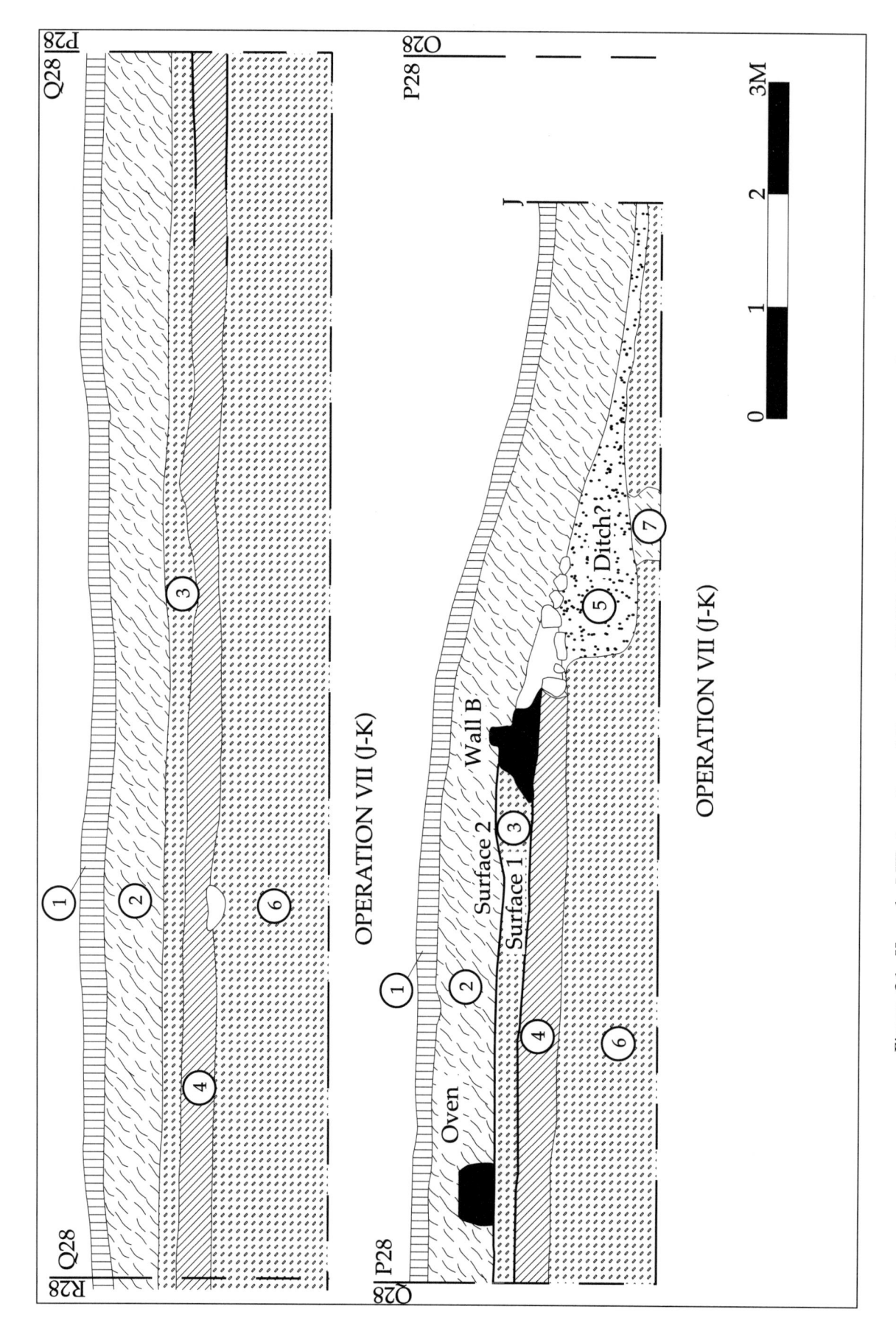

Figure 21. Hasanlu I: West section of Operation VII J-K (P28-R28). See plan, Fig. 26.

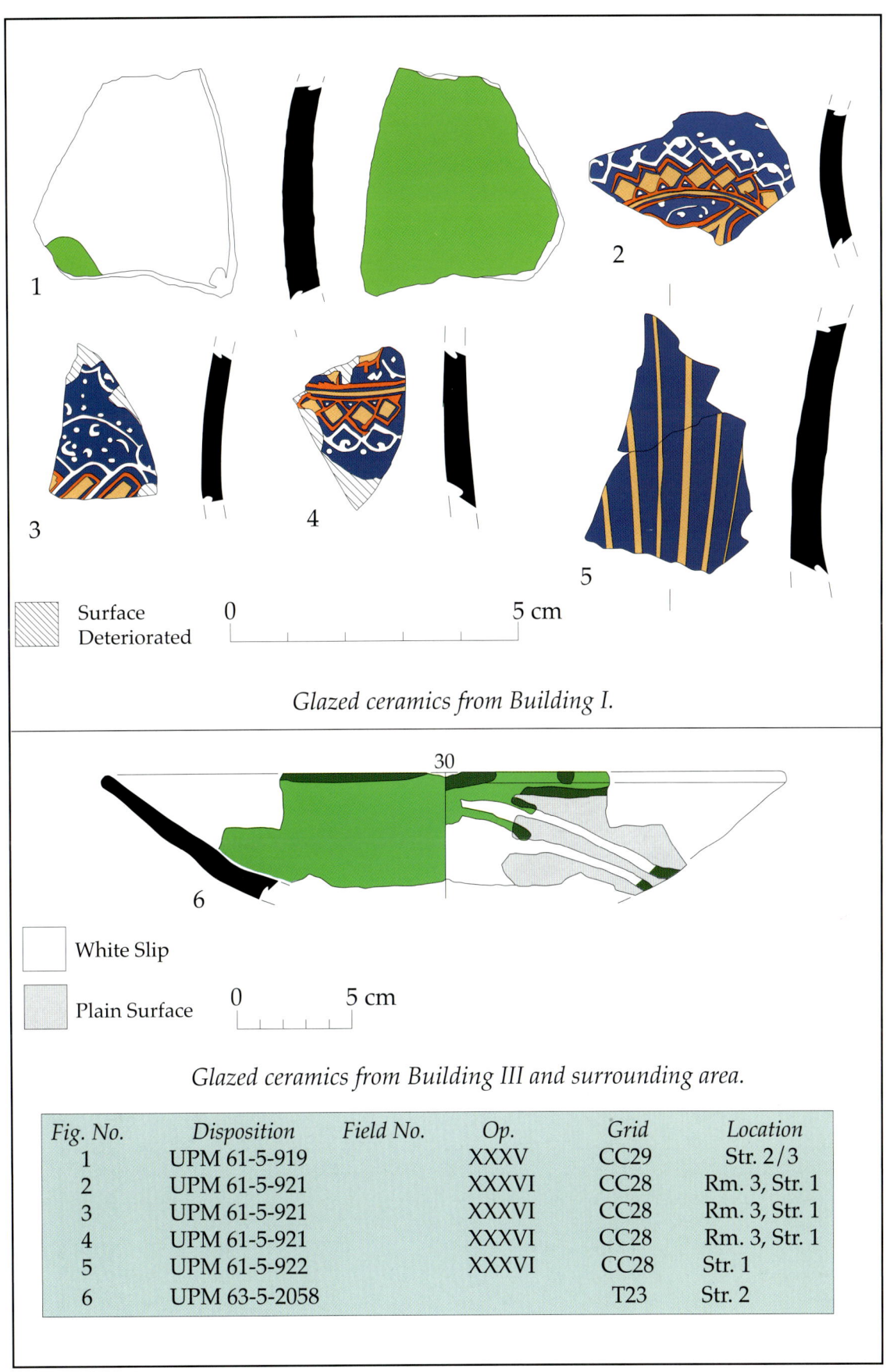

Glazed ceramics from Building I.

Glazed ceramics from Building III and surrounding area.

Fig. No.	Disposition	Field No.	Op.	Grid	Location
1	UPM 61-5-919		XXXV	CC29	Str. 2/3
2	UPM 61-5-921		XXXVI	CC28	Rm. 3, Str. 1
3	UPM 61-5-921		XXXVI	CC28	Rm. 3, Str. 1
4	UPM 61-5-921		XXXVI	CC28	Rm. 3, Str. 1
5	UPM 61-5-922		XXXVI	CC28	Str. 1
6	UPM 63-5-2058			T23	Str. 2

Color Plate A. Hasanlu I: Glazed ceramics from Buildings I and III.

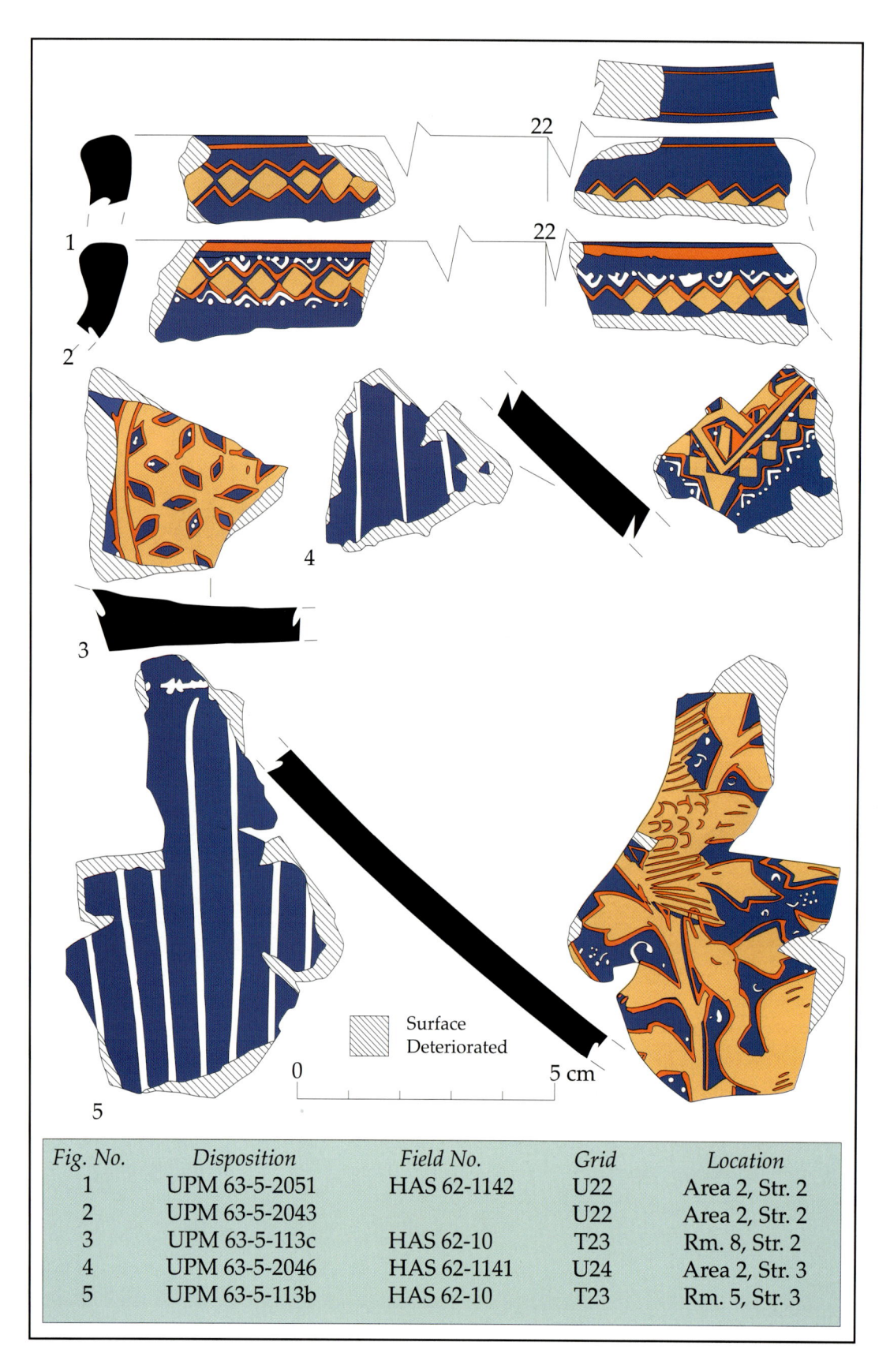

Fig. No.	Disposition	Field No.	Grid	Location
1	UPM 63-5-2051	HAS 62-1142	U22	Area 2, Str. 2
2	UPM 63-5-2043		U22	Area 2, Str. 2
3	UPM 63-5-113c	HAS 62-10	T23	Rm. 8, Str. 2
4	UPM 63-5-2046	HAS 62-1141	U24	Area 2, Str. 3
5	UPM 63-5-113b	HAS 62-10	T23	Rm. 5, Str. 3

Color Plate B. Hasanlu I: Glazed ceramics from Building III and surrounding area.

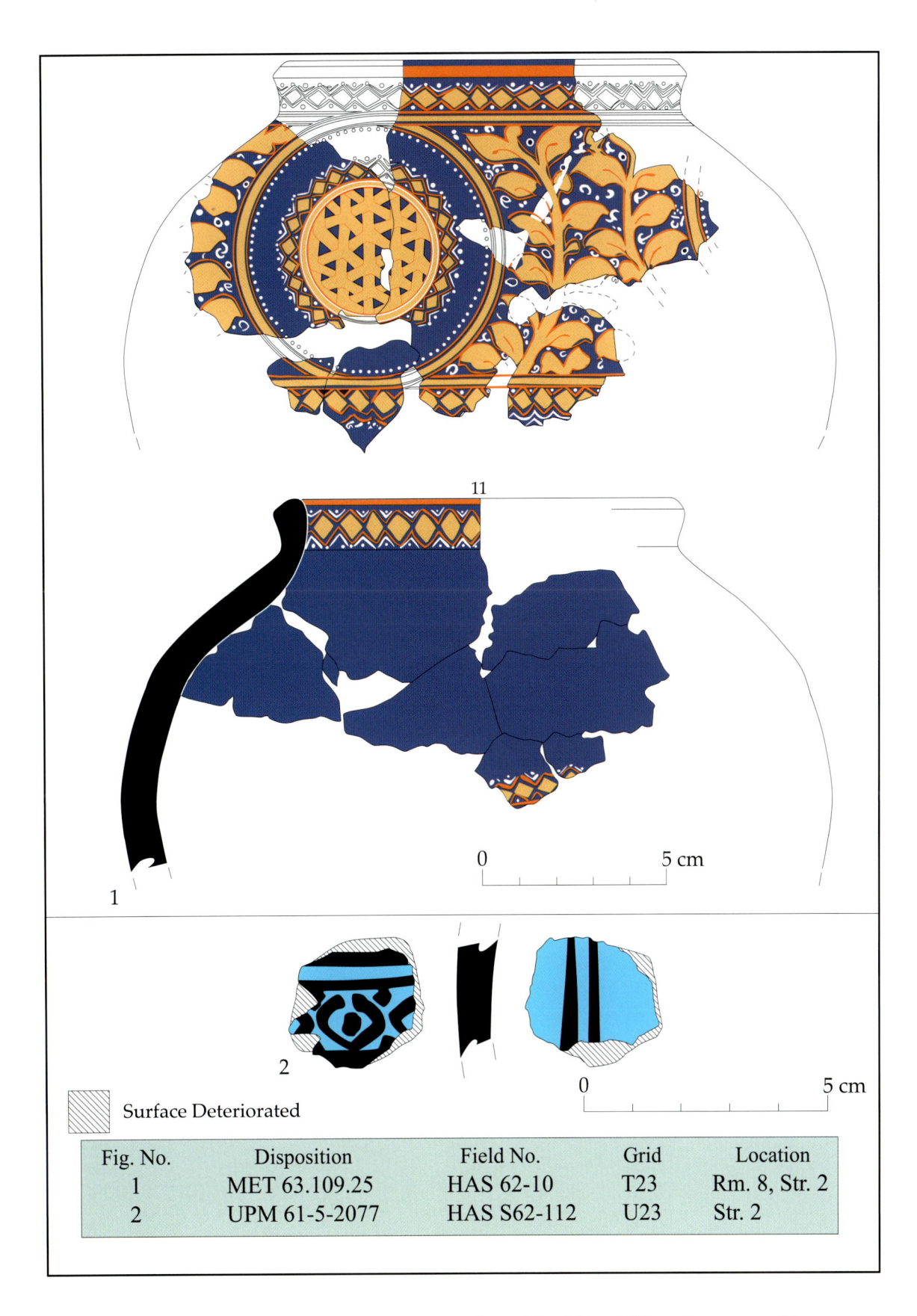

Fig. No.	Disposition	Field No.	Grid	Location
1	MET 63.109.25	HAS 62-10	T23	Rm. 8, Str. 2
2	UPM 61-5-2077	HAS S62-112	U23	Str. 2

Color Plate C. Hasanlu I: Glazed ceramics from Building III and surrounding area.

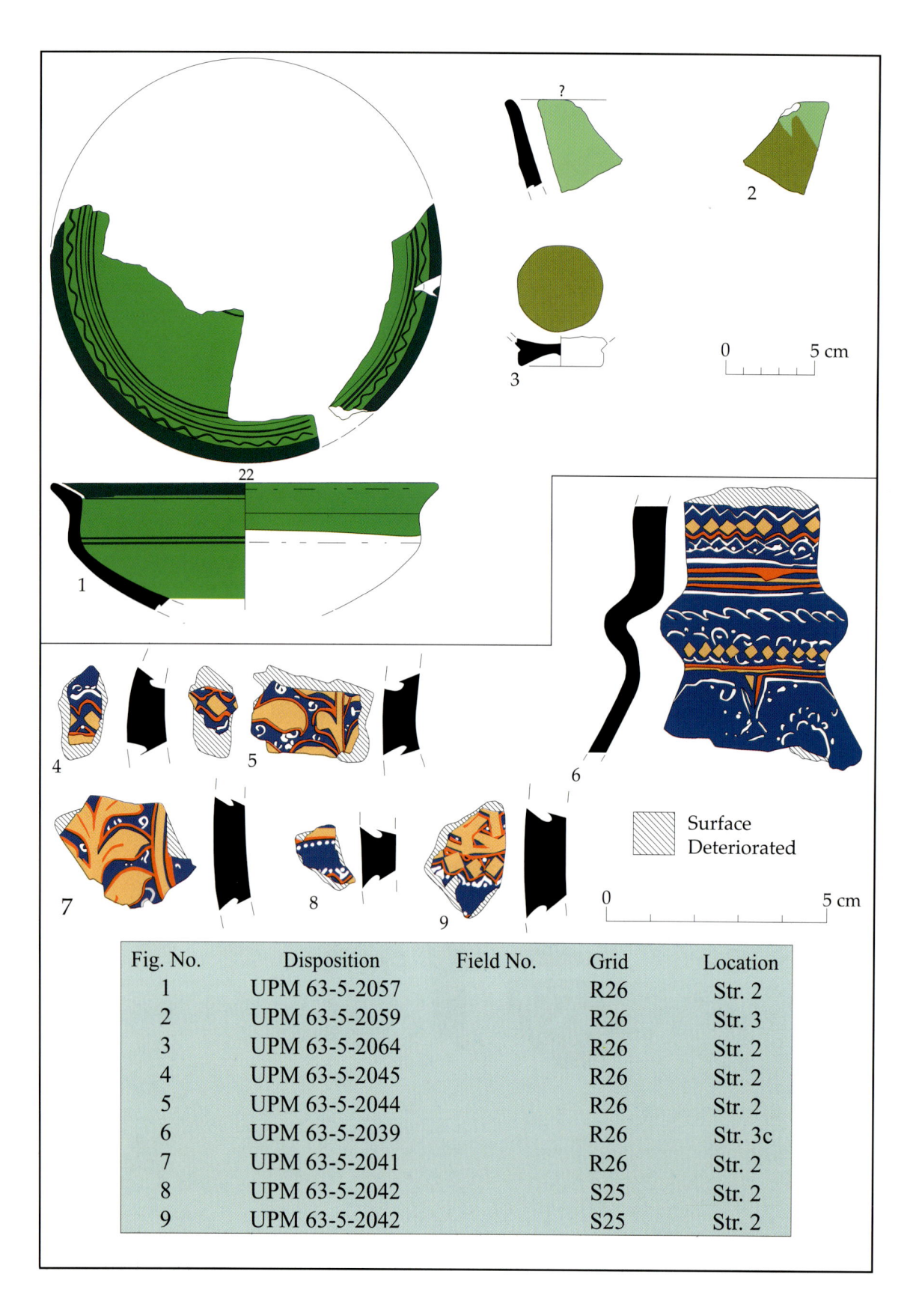

Fig. No.	Disposition	Field No.	Grid	Location
1	UPM 63-5-2057		R26	Str. 2
2	UPM 63-5-2059		R26	Str. 3
3	UPM 63-5-2064		R26	Str. 2
4	UPM 63-5-2045		R26	Str. 2
5	UPM 63-5-2044		R26	Str. 2
6	UPM 63-5-2039		R26	Str. 3c
7	UPM 63-5-2041		R26	Str. 2
8	UPM 63-5-2042		S25	Str. 2
9	UPM 63-5-2042		S25	Str. 2

Color Plate D. Hasanlu I: Glazed ceramics from Building IV and surrounding area.

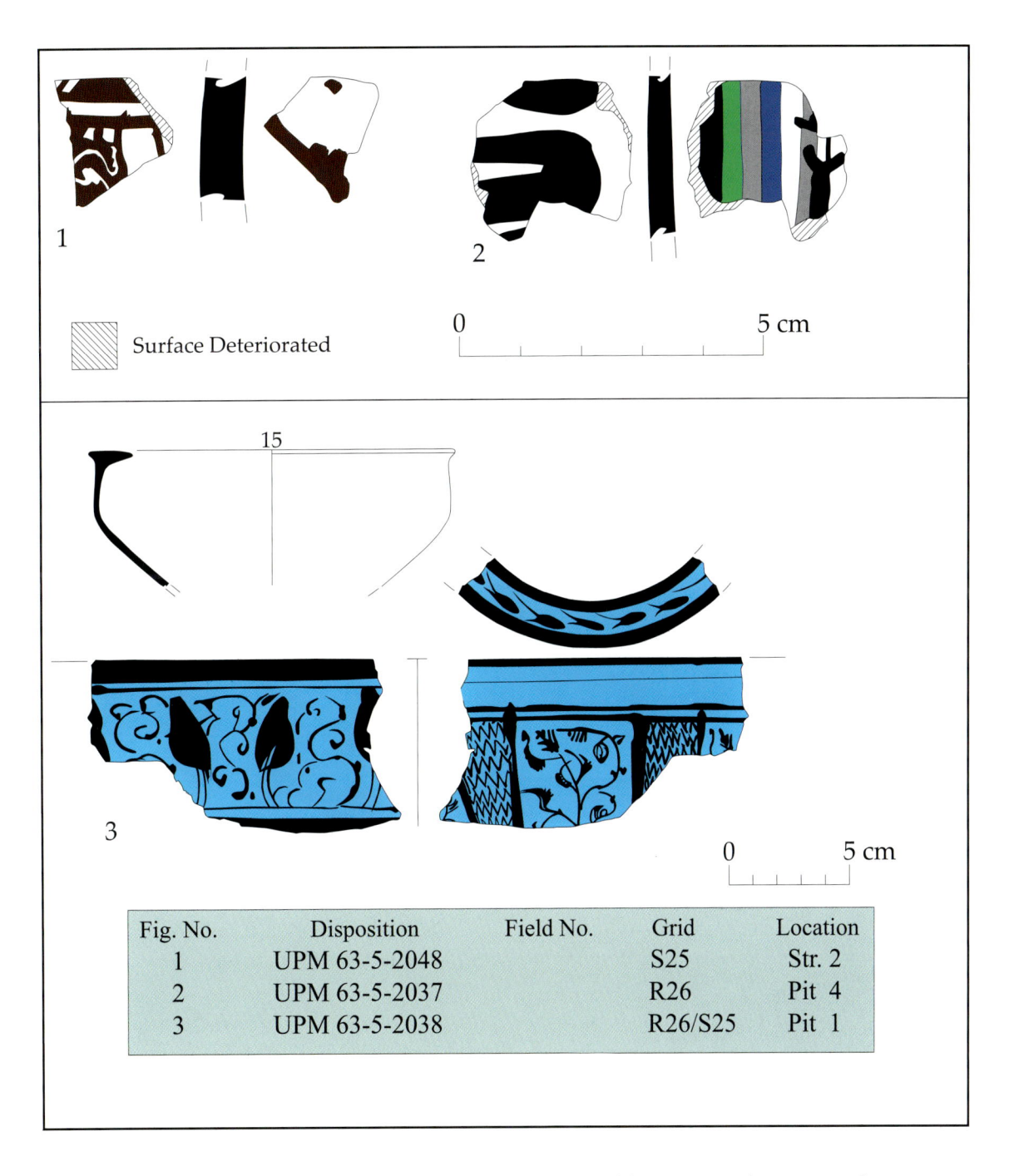

Fig. No.	Disposition	Field No.	Grid	Location
1	UPM 63-5-2048		S25	Str. 2
2	UPM 63-5-2037		R26	Pit 4
3	UPM 63-5-2038		R26/S25	Pit 1

Color Plate E. Hasanlu I: Glazed ceramics from Building IV and surrounding area.

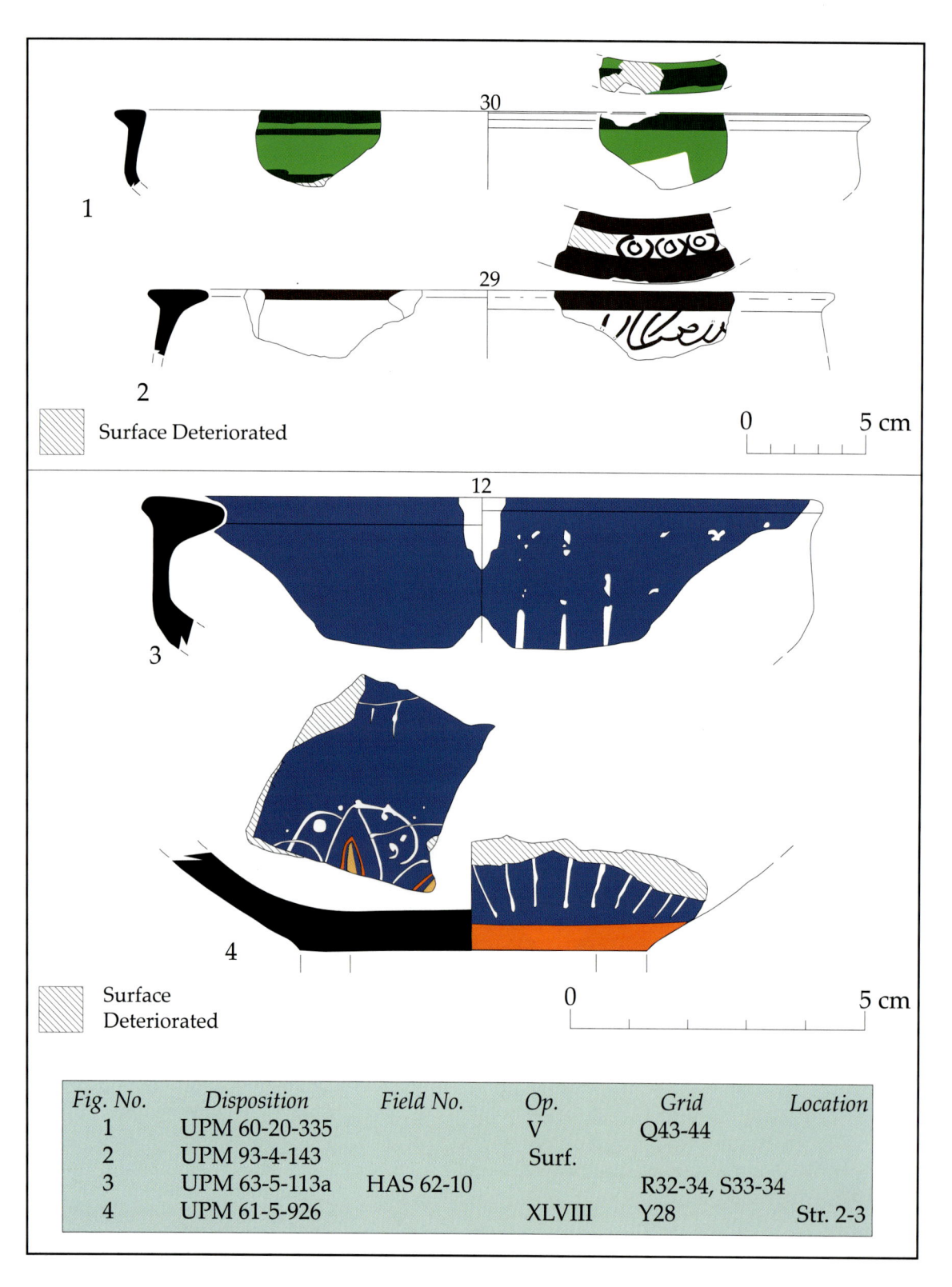

Fig. No.	Disposition	Field No.	Op.	Grid	Location
1	UPM 60-20-335		V	Q43-44	
2	UPM 93-4-143		Surf.		
3	UPM 63-5-113a	HAS 62-10		R32-34, S33-34	
4	UPM 61-5-926		XLVIII	Y28	Str. 2-3

Color Plate F. Hasanlu I: Glazed ceramics from various contexts at Hasanlu Tepe.

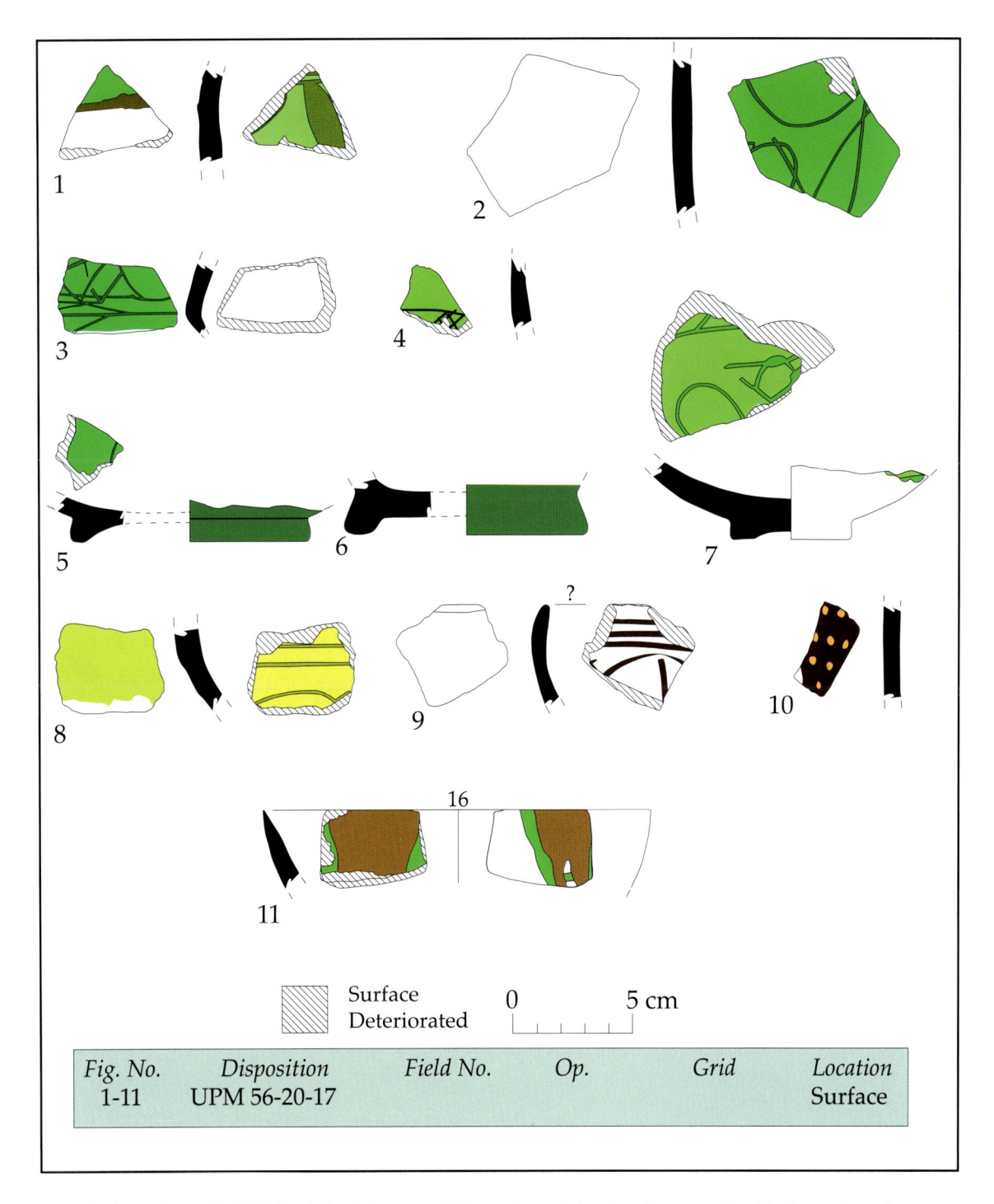

Fig. No.	Disposition	Field No.	Op.	Grid	Location
1-11	UPM 56-20-17				Surface

Color Plate G. Takht-i Sulaimān: Glazed and incised ware (called variously Gerrus Ware, Ghabri Ware, Aghkand Ware, and Amul Ware) from the 1956 Reconnaissance.

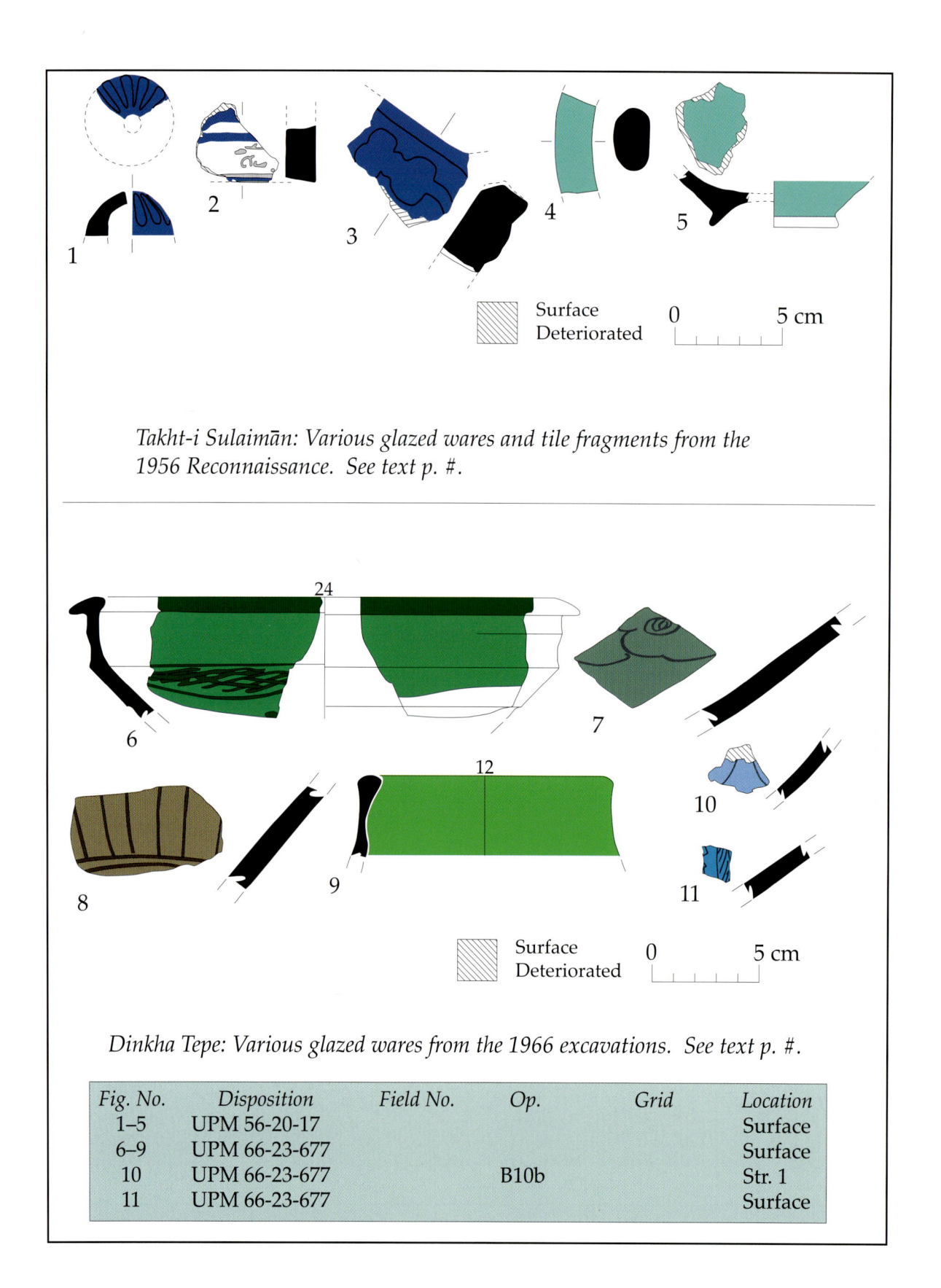

Takht-i Sulaimān: Various glazed wares and tile fragments from the 1956 Reconnaissance. See text p. #.

Dinkha Tepe: Various glazed wares from the 1966 excavations. See text p. #.

Fig. No.	Disposition	Field No.	Op.	Grid	Location
1–5	UPM 56-20-17				Surface
6–9	UPM 66-23-677				Surface
10	UPM 66-23-677		B10b		Str. 1
11	UPM 66-23-677				Surface

Color Plate H. Takht-i Sulaimān and Dinkha Tepe: Various glazed wares.

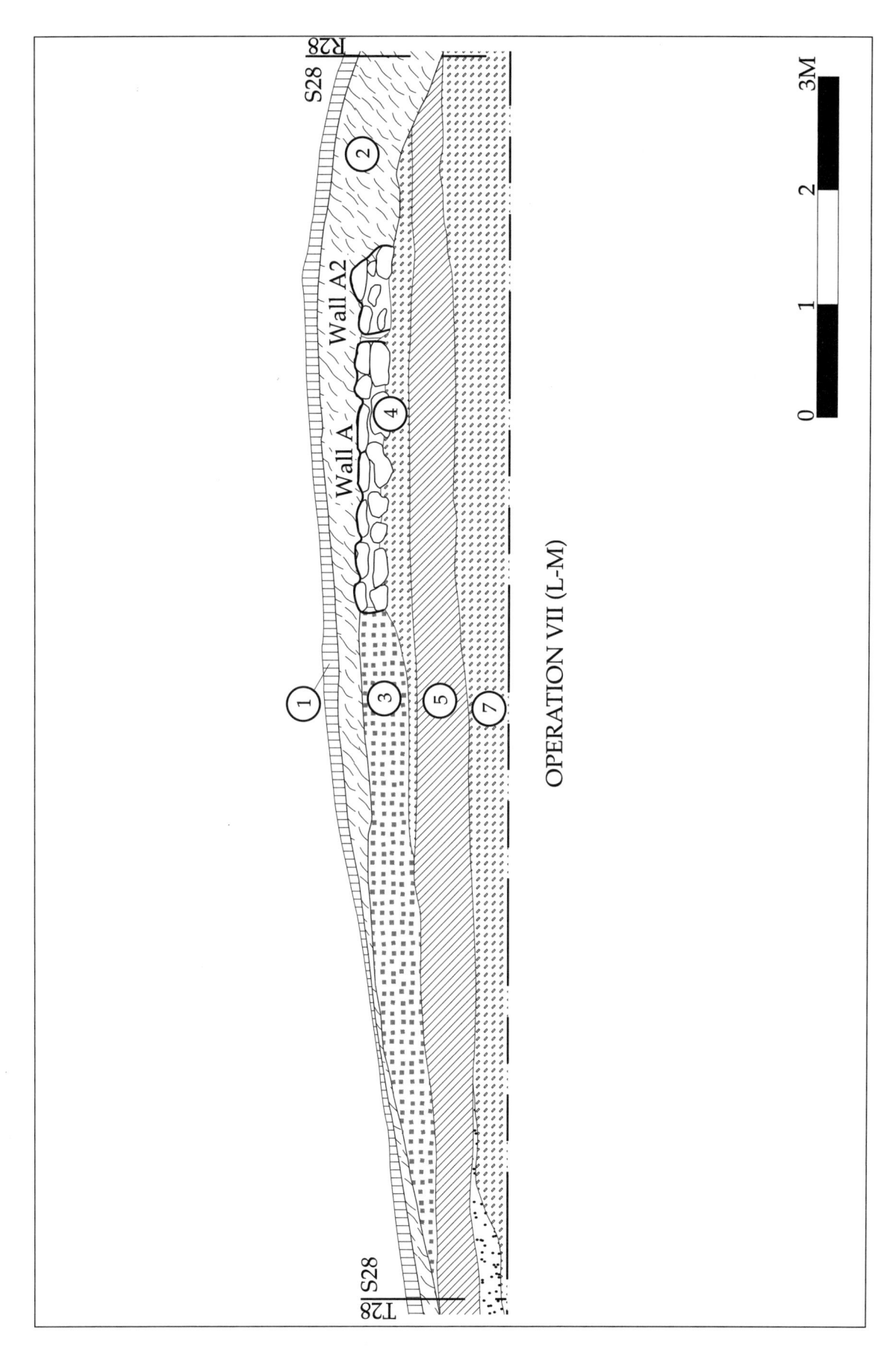

Figure 22. Hasanlu I: West section of Operation VII L-M (O28-T28). See plan Fig. 26.

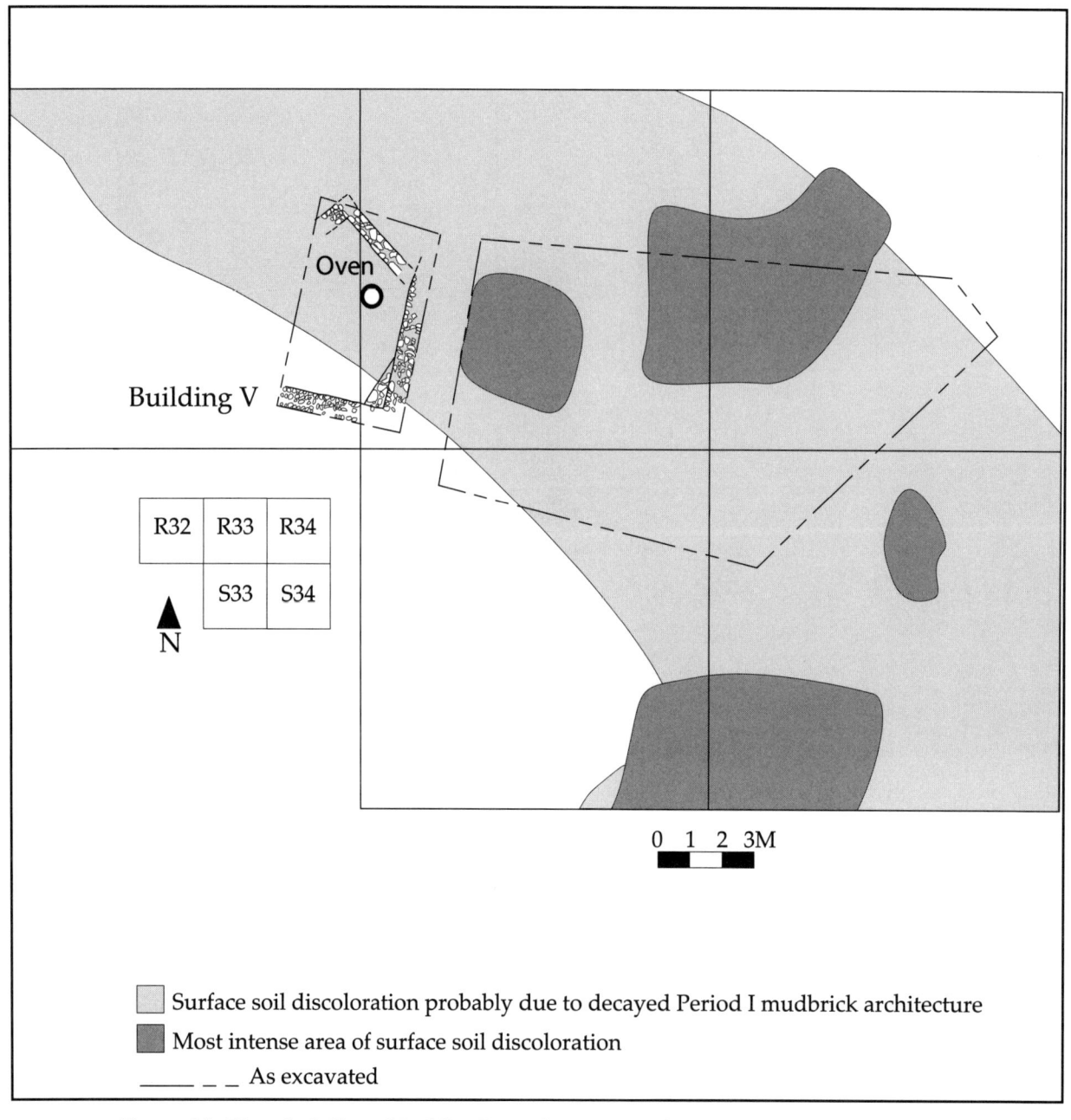

Figure 23. Hasanlu I: Plan of Building V, northeastern High Mound, excavated in 1959.

6

THE NORTHEAST HIGH MOUND

BUILDING V (FIGURES 23-26)

OPERATION L
GRIDS R32-34, S33-34

The expedition uncovered a small portion of a structure, Building V, in Operation L, a 1959 test excavation located over the High Mound's northeast prominence and the surface soil discoloration (Figure 23). Stone footings were visible on the surface in this area at the time of excavation. The excavations revealed the stone footings of two phases of a single room. The earlier phase was oriented northeast to southwest and the later one more north to south. The later phase contained an oven (diameter 75 cm) sunk into the ground and a hearth (the hearth was not mapped). A large scatter of Period I small finds and ceramics was found at the western end of the eastern excavation area (Figures 24-26). This deposit may represent a midden associated with the nearby architecture. If associated with Building V, these objects suggest the area was a domestic space where weaving and food preparation took place. The objects include a fragmentary iron buckle, possibly from a belt or strap, and three fragmentary bracelets (Figure 24:1-4). A cosmetic container, or possibly a small bone handle, is incised with concentric circles and is similar to those of Period IVB (9th century BC) where such containers are fairly common in primary contexts (Figure 24:5). Two pierced cylindrical stones are yellowish in color (Figure 24:6-7; Plate Q). Local villagers informed the excavators that such amulets were traditionally worn by children to ward off illness. A group of three flat bone tools (Figure 24:8-10; Plate Q) showed signs of much wear on their pointed ends and were probably a set of weaving battens, probably a weaving sword, and two shorter pin beaters (Broudy 1979). Other evidence for textile manufacture is a terracotta loom weight and two spindle whorls (Figure 24:11-13; Plate Q). A sherd disc and two rubbing or grinding stones are typical of domestic deposits from most time periods in the Near East (Figure 24:14-16).

With regard to Stein's 1936 sketch map, Building V was aligned to the fortification wall. Operation L lay over, or quite close to, the northeast corner of the inner circumvallation, but the excavators found no sign of the fortification wall or of small, circular bastions or towers unless Building V itself was a square tower at the north end of Stein's entryway.

PERIOD I CERAMICS FROM BUILDING V AND THE SURROUNDING AREA (FIGURES 25-26)

The majority of ceramics from this area were of red or buff ware. The red ware forms include pitchers (Figure 25:1, 2), a small jar (Figure 25:3), a large jar (Figure 25:4), a canteen with pierced lug (Figure 25:5), and a large flat base, probably from a pitcher (Figure 25:6). Buff ware forms are particularly coarse with the exception of a small bowl (Figure 26:1). Two coarse saucer lamps, a lantern (Plate R), and a pot stand or pinch pot (Plate Q) round out the assemblage (Figure 26:2-5). The only other Period I lamp, also in buff ware, was found on the southern High Mound and was spouted (Figure 27:5). A single glazed jar sherd was found with deteriorated green and yellow glaze (Figure 26:6). The absence of finer glazed wares from this area is noteworthy.

FIGURE 24. HASANLU I: SMALL FINDS FROM BUILDING V AND SURROUNDING AREA

Fig. No.	Disposition	Field No.	Material	Artifact Type and Description	Dimensions	Op.	Grid	Location
1	Discarded	HAS 59-332	Iron	Buckle	l. 6.5 cm, w. 1.5 cm, th. 0.8 cm	L	R32-34, S33-34	Str. 2
2	TM	HAS 59-334a	Glass	Yellow-olive bracelet	d. 0.5 cm, l. 4.5 cm	L	R32-34, S33-34	Str. 2
3	Discarded	HAS 59-334b	Cu/Bronze	Bracelet	d. 0.3 cm, l. 2.2 cm	L	R32-34, S33-34	Str. 2
4	Discarded	HAS 59-334c	Iron	Bracelet	d. 0.9 cm, l. 6.5 cm	L	R32-34, S33-34	Str. 2
5	UPM 60-20-18	HAS 59-337	Bone	Incised handle	l. 6.5 cm, w. 2.1 cm, th. 1.0 cm	L	R32-34, S33-34	Str. 2
6	UPM 60-20-47	HAS 59-336a	Stone	Yellow amulet	l. 5.0 cm, w. 2.1 cm, th. 1.0 cm	L	R32-34, S33-34	Str. 2
7	TM	HAS 59-336b	Stone	Yellow amulet	l. 3.2 cm, w. 2.5 cm	L	R32-34, S33-34	Str. 2
8	UPM 60-20-306	HAS 59-333a	Bone	Weaving implement	l. 8.5 cm, w. 1.9 cm, th. 0.2 cm	L	R32-34, S33-34	Str. 2
9	TM	HAS 59-333b	Bone	Weaving implement	l. 10.3 cm, w. 2.2 cm, th. 0.2 cm	L	R32-34, S33-34	Str. 2
10	Discarded	HAS 59-333c	Bone	Weaving implement	l. 34 cm, w. 2.6 cm, th. 0.2 cm	L	R32-34, S33-34	Str. 2
11	Discarded	HAS 59-329	Terracotta	Loom weight	l. 3.4 cm, w. 3.3 cm, th. 3.0 cm	L	R32-34, S33-34	Str. 2
12	TM	HAS 59-338	Terracotta	Spindle whorl	l. 4.3 cm, w. 3.1 cm, th. 4.5, hole d. 0.5 cm	L	R32-34, S33-34	Str. 2
13	UPM 60-20-302	HAS 59-340	Bone	Boss	d. 3.0 cm, th. 1.1 cm	L	R32-34, S33-34	Area 1
14	Discarded	HAS 59-335	Terracotta	Disc	d. 2.5 cm, th. 0.6 cm	L	R32-34, S33-34	Str. 2
15	Discarded	HAS 59-339	Stone	Rubbing stone	l. 5.6 cm, w. 3.5 cm, th. 3.5 cm	L	R32-34, S33-34	Str. 2
16	Discarded	HAS 59-328	Basalt	Grinder	l. 10 cm, w. 8.9 cm, th. 4.5 cm	L	R32-34, S33-34	Str. 2

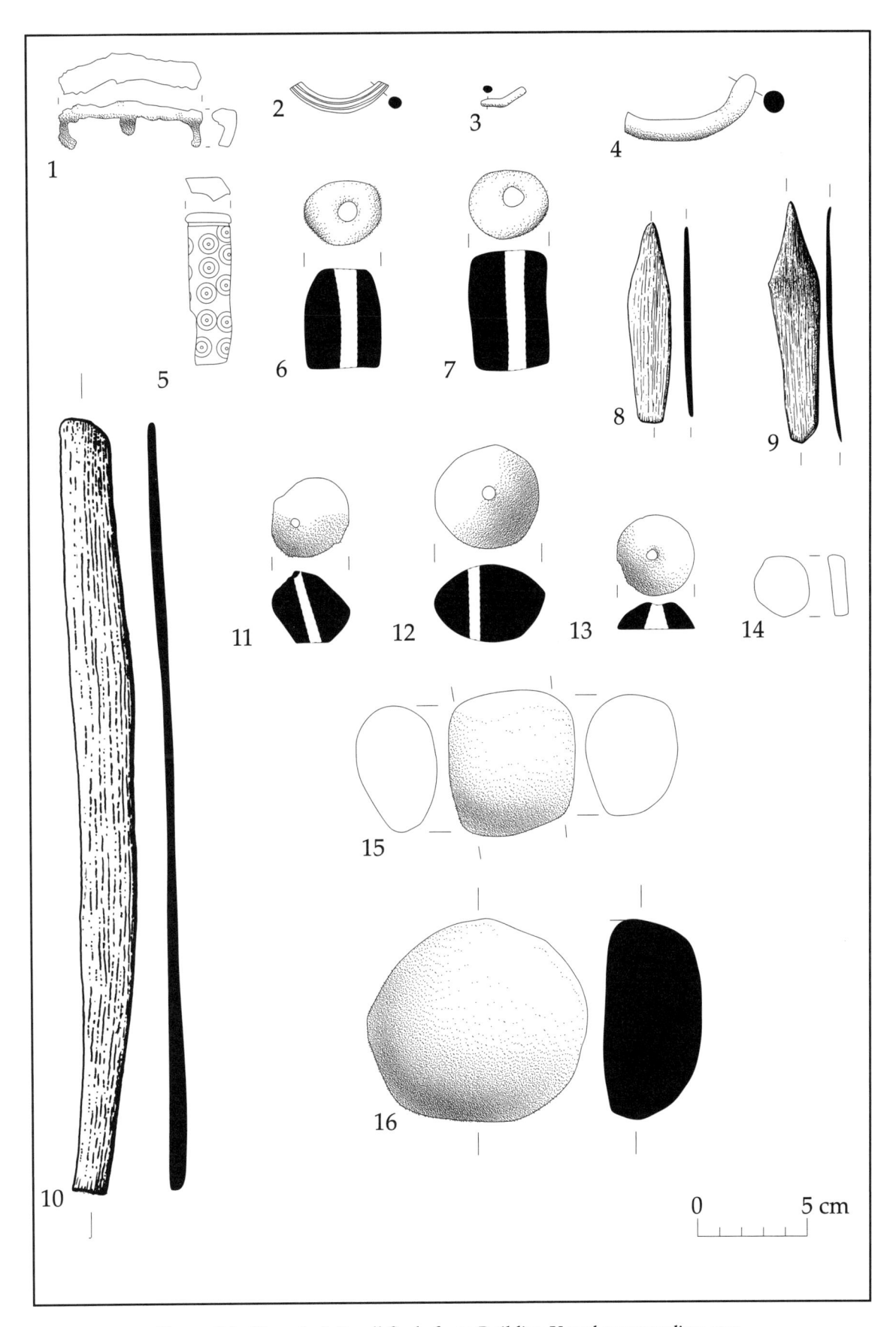

Figure 24. Hasanlu I: Small finds from Building V and surrounding area.

Figure 25. Hasanlu I: Red Ware Ceramics from Building V and Surrounding Area

Fig. No.	Disposition	Field No.	Op.	Grid	Location
1	UPM 60-20-340		L	R32-34, S33-34	Str. 2
2	UPM 60-20-332		L	R32-34, S33-34	Str. 2
3	UPM 60-20-333		L	R32-34, S33-34	Str. 2
4	UPM 60-20-339		L	R32-34, S33-34	Str. 2
5	UPM 60-20-336		L	R32-34, S33-34	Str. 2
6	Discarded		L	R32-34, S33-34	Str. 2

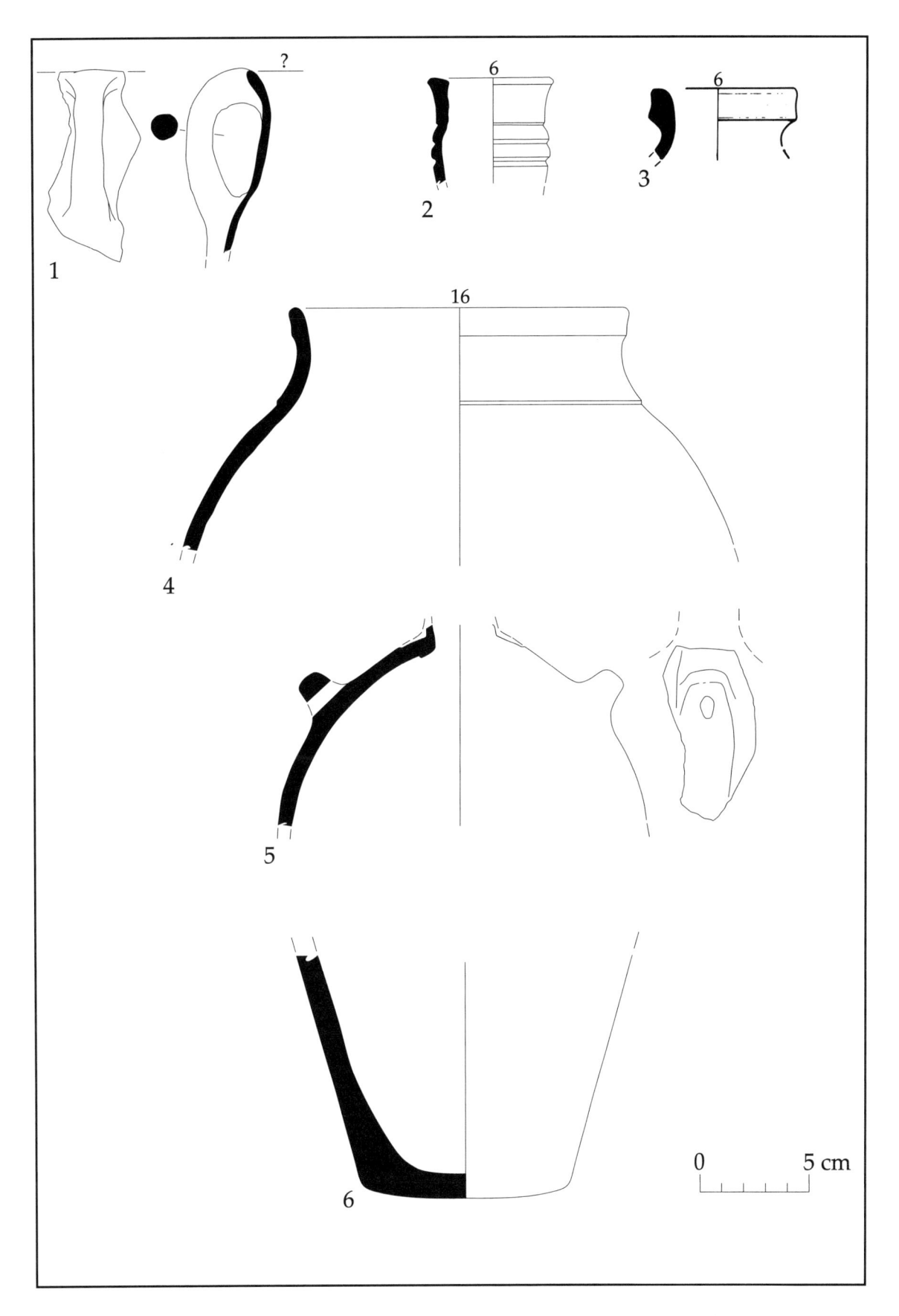

Figure 25. Hasanlu I: Red ware ceramics from Building V and surrounding area.

Figure 26. Hasanlu I: Ceramics from Building V and Surrounding Area

Fig. No.	Disposition	Field No.	Op.	Grid	Location
1	TM 10913	HAS 59-341	L	R32-34, S33-34	Area 1, Str. 1a
2	Discarded	HAS 59-326	L	R32-34, S33-34	Str. 2
3	Discarded	HAS 59-327	L	R32-34, S33-34	Str. 2
4	Discarded	HAS 59-331	L	R32-34, S33-34	Str. 2
5	Discarded	HAS 59-330	L	R32-34, S33-34	Str. 2
6	UPM 60-20-330		L	R32-34, S33-34	Str. 2

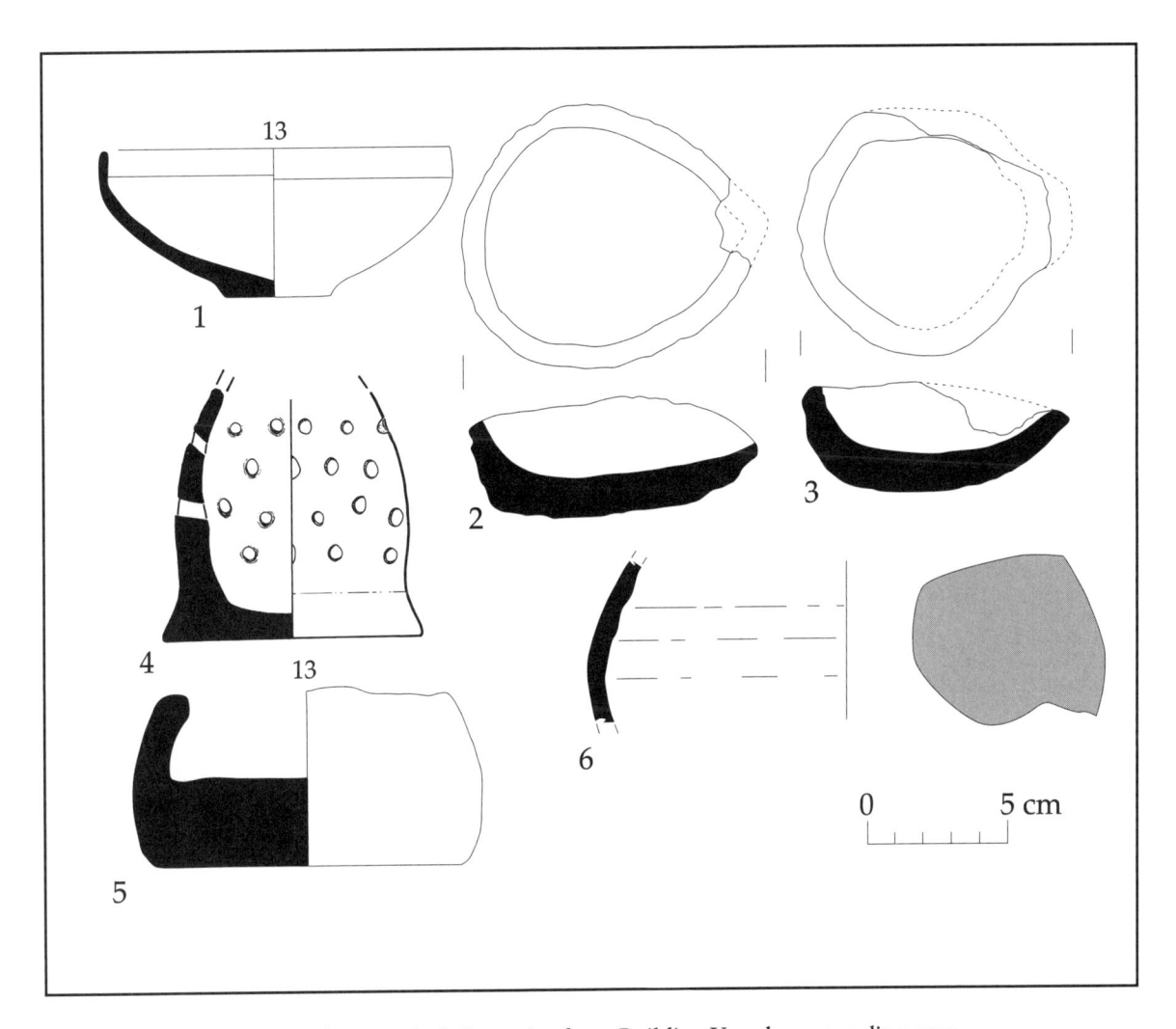

Figure 26. Hasanlu I: Ceramics from Building V and surrounding area.

FIGURE 27. HASANLU I: CERAMICS FROM VARIOUS CONTEXTS

Fig. No.	Disposition	Field No.	Op.	Grid	Location
1	UPM 93-1-149		Surf		
2	UPM 61-5-927		XLIII	Y28	Str. 2-3
3	UPM 93-4-144		IX F-G		
4	UPM 60-20-337		XIX	BB26	
5	UPM 59-4-2111	HAS 58-112	IX R-L		
6	UPM 61-5-928		XLIII	Y28	Str. 2
7	UPM 60-20-328		XVIII	BB27	Str. 1-2

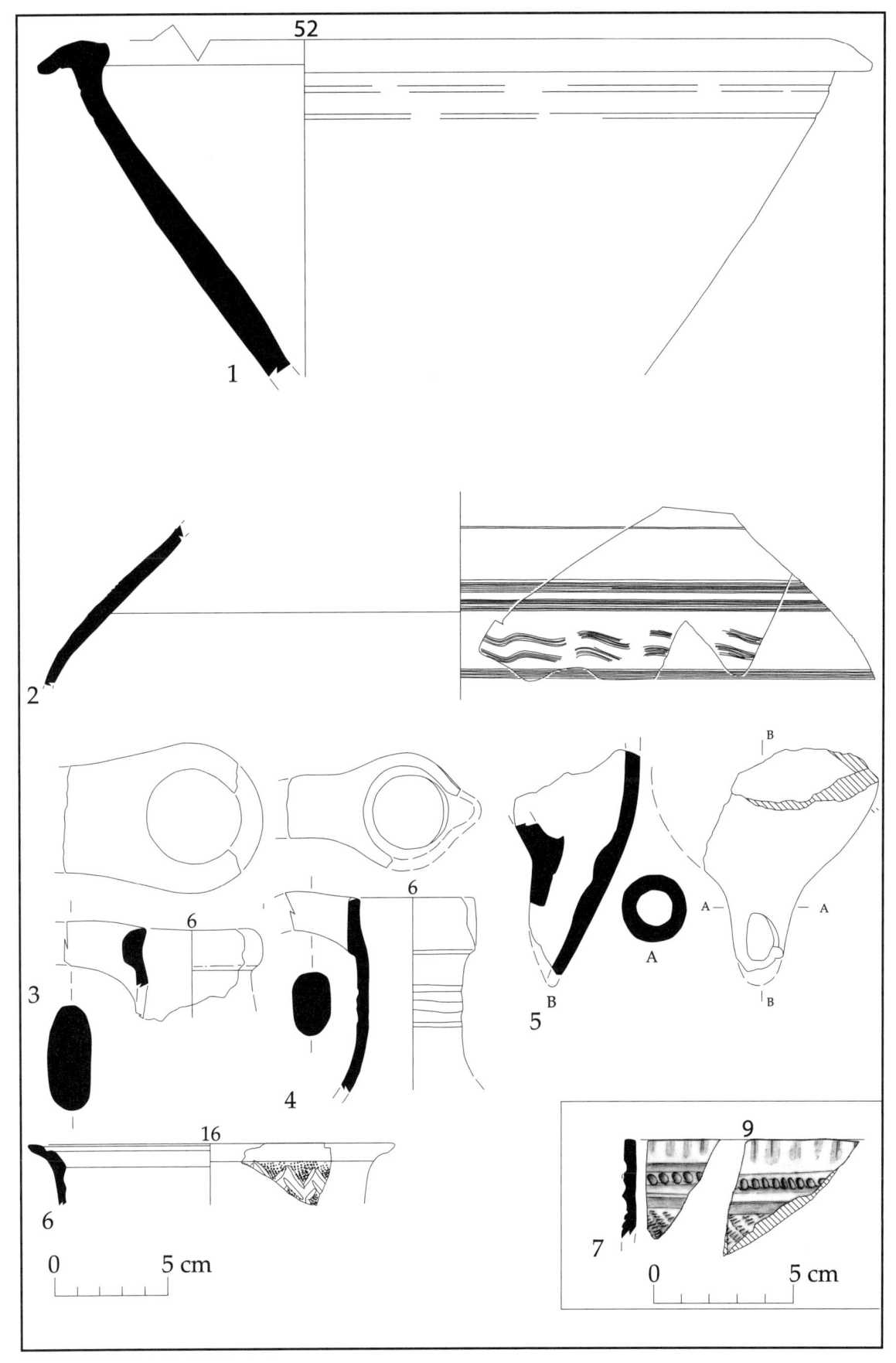

Figure 27. Hasanlu I: Ceramics from various contexts.

7

REGIONAL RECONNAISSANCE, SURVEYS, AND EXCAVATIONS

In 1956, Dyson collected ceramic diagnostics roughly contemporary to Hasanlu Period I during a reconnaissance of archaeological sites conducted in northern and western Iran. By far the most important site of this period was Takht-i Sulaimān, probably the Parthian Praaspa, capital of Media Atropatene (Wilber 1938; Cassius Dio XLIX, 25-28) the famous Sasanian sanctuary of *Jis* (Arabic *Shīz*) of Ādur Gushnasp, *Sughūrlūq* or *Saturiq* to the Mongols (Crane 1937; Boyle 1968:367).* The German Archaeological Institute worked at the site from 1959 to 1978 under the direction of Rudolf Naumann. Most of the Ilkhanid architecture exposed at the site was monumental in character, and so offers limited assistance in the interpretation of the relatively modest remains from Hasanlu. The division of space seen in Hasanlu Buildings I and III is analogous to the four *aivān* structures with cruciform central spaces typical of both monumental and vernacular architecture at Takht-i Sulaimān (Masuya 1997:116-56). Like Hasanlu Building I, the central court of some of these structures lay at a lower level than the surrounding rooms, such as the Cruciform Room and the Residential Complex of Area T8 (Masuya 1997:144-45, 147-48). Ovens used in the residential areas of the *Takht* appear to be identical to those of Hasanlu I, for example those in the so-called Farm Complex Rooms 11 and 12 and the ovens in Area XA-XF (Masuya 1997:142-43, 147-48).

The final publication of the ceramics from the *Takht* is pending (cf. Allan 1974:16), but some material has been published in preliminary reports, short articles (Schnyder 1972, 1974), and exhibit catalogs (Naumann and Naumann 1976; Komaroff and Carboni 2002). The main phases of occupation date to the Achaemenid, Parthian, Sasanian, Saljūq, and Ilkhanid periods. During the Ilkhanid period, the *Takht* was the site of an ornately decorated summer residence of the Il-Khan Abaqa (r. 1265-1281 AD) constructed after 1270 atop the remains of the Sasanian fire temple. Abaqa dwelt there only three summers. Later, Öljeitü (r. 1303-16) made his summer residence at Sulṭānīyeh (Naumann 1974:198-99; Blair 1986a; Kleiss 1997), founded by his predecessor Arghun (r. 1284-91).

The University of Pennsylvania Museum currently has in its collections 37 diagnostic sherds from the site (UPM 56-20-17 nos. 1-37). Nearly all of this material may be dated to the Saljūq and Ilkhanid occupation. The assemblage bears a striking resemblance to Hasanlu Period I; all the major ware groups are represented with the exception of Hasanlu I buff ware. Red ware from Takht-i Sulaimān is virtually identical to that from Hasanlu I in terms of paste and temper. However, the two reconstructable forms available from Takht-i Sulaimān have no parallels at Hasanlu (Figure 28:1, 2). Like Hasanlu, comb-incising in bands and wavy-lines is attested, as is impressed decoration (Figure 28:3, 4).

Hasanlu's monochrome green-glazed ware has parallels with a group of ceramics commonly referred to as "Garrus Ware" (Naumann and Naumann 1976:33, Pls. 3-4). Varieties of such *sgraffiato*-decorated glazed wares, typically bowl forms, have an

---

* The site is identified as Saturiq by Ḥamd Allāh Mustaufī Qazvīnī (1915-19).

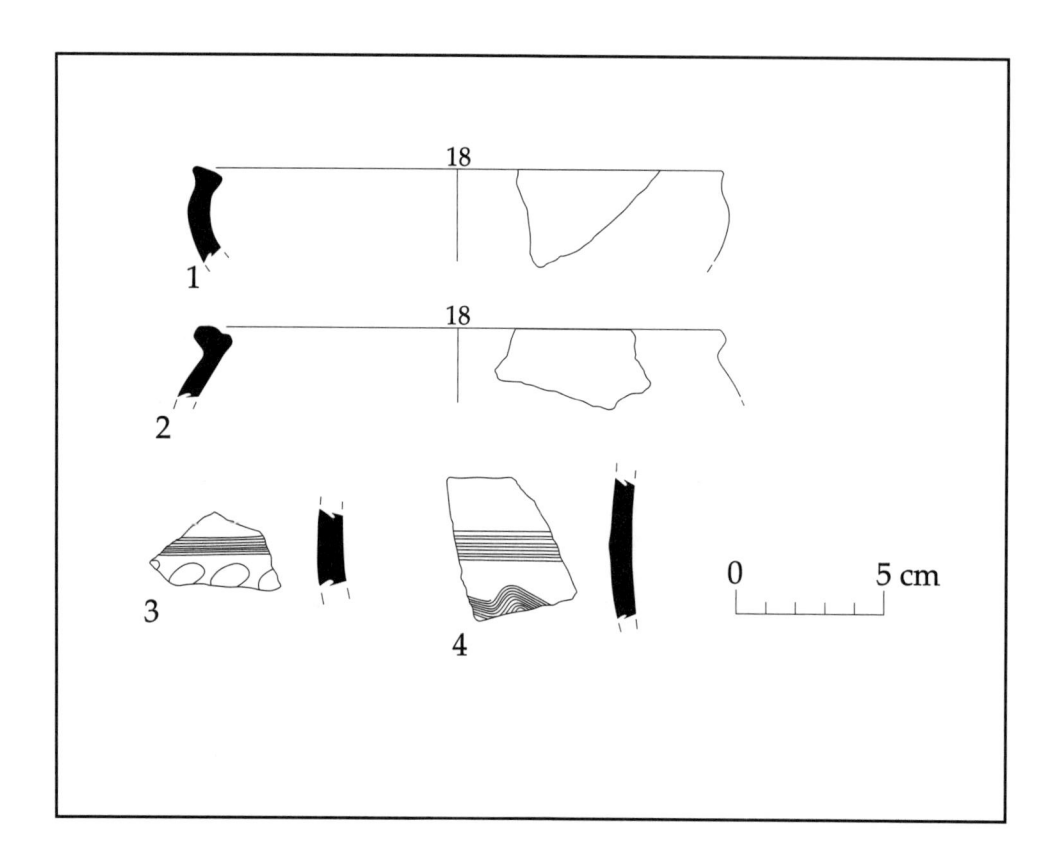

Figure 28. Takht-i Sulaimān: Red ware ceramics from the 1956 Reconnaissance.

extremely wide distribution in the Near East and eastern Mediterranean, but are especially common from the environs of Tabrīz to the region south of the Caspian Sea, where such wares are fairly well known from archaeological surveys in the region dominated by the Ismāʿīlīs (Assassins) from 1091 to the late 1250s AD (Naumann and Naumann 1976; Kleiss 1985; Willey 1963).

Scholars have coined a plethora of ware names to distinguish the regional and temporal variations of *sgraffiato* and champlevé (excised) decorated wares, including Āmul Ware, Aghkand Ware, and Garrus Ware (also known as Ghabri Ware). These styles of ceramics are typically made of red earthenware covered in a white or pinkish-buff slip. The slip often does not extend all the way down to the base on the exterior of vessels, or it may be painted on to create an underglaze design. Vessels typically have incised and/or excised decoration in a wide variety of motifs. Glazes are clear or colored; typical colors are green, pale yellow, golden yellow to golden brown, and manganese purple. Glaze may be applied in the incised and excised design to highlight it, or incising may be used to surround glazed areas to prevent the glaze from running. Alternatively, the entire vessel may be glazed. The incised and excised designs appear much darker due to the pooling of glaze in these areas and the removal of the underlying white slip. Often the glaze does not extend to the base of the vessel on the exterior or is haphazardly applied there. Rims and bases are often given a thick coating of glaze. Another common decorative technique involves the use of splash glazing, typically in green and golden brown.

According to the excavators, the glazed *sgraffiato* of Takht-i Sulaimān dates to the 12th to late 13th centuries (i.e., the Saljūq to early Mongol Periods)—the latter part of the Zwischenzeit (10th to mid 13th centuries AD, Naumann and Naumann 1976:32-33, nos. 80-95). Schnyder has posited that monochrome glazed yellow and green *sgraffiato* is a spatio-temporal indicator of Saljūq expansion and does not appear before the second half of the 11th century (1972:194-97; but see also Allan 1974:20). The continuation of these wares into the latter 13th and 14th centuries has received much less attention.

In comparison with Hasanlu, a wider range of glaze colors and design techniques was employed at Takht-i Sulaimān. Champlevé and incising occur in monochrome green-glazed ware (Color Plate G:1), but champlevé is unattested at Hasanlu, and there appears to be a reduction in the frequency of incised vessels and the amount of incising. The small number of incised designs from Hasanlu seem to be more precise and regularized (Color Plate D:1, Color Plate F:1). The Takht-i Sulaimān incised motifs are usually geometric and abstract (Color Plate G:2, 7; cf. Schnyder 1972:195); vessels are often covered with incised bands filled with cross-hatching (Color Plate G:3, 4; Naumann and Naumann 1976:pl. 3, nos. 80, 89). Yellow, purple, and golden brown glazes were also used at Takht-i Sulaimān (Color Plate G:8-11), but are wholly absent at Hasanlu. Other techniques unattested at Hasanlu are the infilling of incision with glaze such as Color Plate G:9 glazed in golden-brown and covered in a clear overglaze on the interior and 3 mm below the rim on the exterior, the painting of designs in white slip to produce an underglaze design (Color Plate G:10) and the use of splash glazing in multiple colors (Color Plate G:11; cf. Naumann and Naumann 1976:pl. 4, nos. 90, 95).

Most of the published examples of Garrus Ware from Takht-i Sulaimān are dated to the 12th to late 13th centuries, but they are not directly linked to late 13th century contexts. Based on an assessment of the limited archaeological evidence from Āzarbaijān, Iran, northern Syria, and Turkey for this period, Allan dates the floruit of these wares to the 11th and 12th centuries (Allan 1974). The occurrence of monochrome green-glazed ware at Hasanlu with lājvardīnah ware in sealed contexts of short duration would seem to expand the time range of at least one variety of these glazed earthenwares to the late 13th and 14th centuries AD. In other areas, this ware, produced at local centers, comes to an end with the Mongol conquest, but at Hasanlu it occurs with a ceramic type closely associated with the Ilkhanid period in a newly founded settlement. The Mongols spared Āzarbaijān much of the destruction they wrought on neighboring areas, and the region was likely the focus of resettlement efforts in the Ilkhanid period to promote rural economic development in the heartland of the new empire (see below). Thus, it is perhaps not surprising to find the survival of pre-Mongol ceramic styles there, whereas in other areas there is a major break with previous traditions.

Other wares among the surface material from Takht-i Sulaimān are stone paste wares covered in cobalt blue (Color Plate H:1, 3) and turquoise-blue glazes (Color Plate H:4, 5). These pieces may have originally been decorated with overglaze decoration now eroded away. Color Plate H:1 is likely a fragmentary spout from a heavy pear-shaped bottle (also called a sphero-conical flask).

Overglaze decoration is well known from Takht-i Sulaimān, primarily from the tile decoration (Naumann 1963, 1971; Naumann and Naumann 1969, 1976). Only one object collected in 1956, part of the lowest register of a frieze tile, retains traces of overglaze decoration in the form of an inscription executed in luster (Color Plate H:2). A complete tile in the Los Angeles County Museum of Art (M.73.5.222) and another in the Walters Art Museum, Baltimore (48.1296), are similar to this fragment. They are attributed to the *Takht* based on excavated fragments from the site made from the same mold but glazed all in blue (Masuya 2002:97-99, figs. 107 and 109; 265-66, cat. nos. 95, 96 with references).

Although only a small fragment, the UPM piece provides additional evidence for attributing these and similar tile depicting scenes from the *Shāhnāma* stories of Faridun and Bahram Gur to the *Takht*, being virtually identical in terms of color scheme, style and extant proportions. The tile fragment shown in Color Plate H:3 would originally have been decorated with luster and almost certainly formed part of the tile revetment of the West Iwan. It is identical to a double pentagonal tile from the site that shows two flying geese. The relief design element on the example at the UPM appears on a complete example of identical color (cf. Masuya 2000:92, fig. 93, the lower of the two double pentagonal tiles, left pentagon, upper right corner).

Underglaze painted ware was also found during the reconnaissance, albeit in small fragments. Examples include Sulṭānābād Ware painted in black, turquoise blue, and cobalt blue (similar to Naumann and Naumann 1976:fig. 18, no. 104) and a ware with black paint under a translucent blue glaze—identical in fabric and color scheme to the example from Hasanlu included here (Color Plate E:3).

On the whole, the ceramics from the later periods of Takht-i Sulaimān provide close comparisons to Hasanlu Period I. Perhaps telling in terms of chronology, many styles of glazed earthenwares common to the 11th to early 13th century levels at Takht-i Sulaimān are absent at Hasanlu, but are found at neighboring sites. While analysis of the Islamic material collected during regional surveys and excavations in the Hasanlu region is ongoing, glazed sgraffiato earthenwares from Hajji Firuz Tepe and Dinkha Tepe closely match the Takht-i Sulaimān assemblage (Figure 1; Voigt 1983; Danti forthcoming).

Dinkha Tepe is located on the banks of the Gadār River in the Ushnu valley approximately 30 km west of Hasanlu (Figure 2). The site was first reported by Sir Aurel Stein (1940:367-76) after his visit in 1936 (Figure 2) and was excavated for two seasons by the Hasanlu Project in 1966 and 1968. Hajji Firuz Tepe lies 2 km southeast of Hasanlu Tepe. The site was excavated by the Hasanlu Project for four seasons, in 1958, 1960, 1961, and 1968 (Voigt 1976, 1983). A radiocarbon date from Hajji Firuz (Lab no. P-1838, 1080±50 AD) supports a Saljūq date for its Islamic material (Voigt 1983:348).

Material from the surface and near-surface strata of Dinkha Tepe is difficult to date with precision but falls somewhere in the 11th to 13th centuries. The range of variation in the monochrome glazed ware assemblage closely resembles that of Takht-i Sulaimān. A green-glazed hammered rim bowl decorated with incised lozenges filled with crosshatching is typical of Garrus Ware (Color Plate H:6). Similar examples were found at Hajji Firuz. Abstract floral designs (Color Plate H:7) are also attested. Other glaze colors represented are golden brown, apple green, turquoise blue, and cobalt blue (Color Plate H:8-11).

It would appear that Hasanlu was probably not occupied in the Saljūq period, although a late Saljūq to early Ilkhanid date cannot be completely rejected. Other sites in the immediate vicinity of Hasanlu, such as Hajji Firuz Tepe and Dinkha Tepe, have assemblages indicating Saljūq settlement at, or nearby, these mounds. While these ceramic assemblages have affinities to Hasanlu, they more closely resemble published ceramics from Takht-i Sulaimān and other material of Saljūq date.

8

SUMMARY AND CONCLUSIONS

The excavated exposure of Hasanlu I, while limited in terms of size, preservation, and the unsystematic collection of ceramics, provides a valuable glimpse of a prosperous rural settlement at the edge of the Ilkhanid heartland of northwestern Iran. With the exception of monumental architecture, this period is poorly known archaeologically in the Near East. Substantive archaeological reports have been published for a small number of sites in Iran, including Takht-i Sulaimān (see esp. Naumann and Naumann 1976; Naumann 1977) and Ghubayrā (Bivar 2000), and in Iraq, most notably Harbâ (Rougeulle 2001), Nippur (Gibson, Armstrong, and McMahon 1998), and Wasiṭ (Safar 1945). In eastern Turkey, a small fortress of the Ilkhanid period was excavated at Taşkun Kale (McNicoll 1983).

Following a hiatus of settlement at the site lasting some 1400 years, the Hasanlu I occupation was probably of short duration. The excavators found evidence for one major construction phase followed by a phase of rebuilding in all the better-preserved structures. The site appears to have been a planned settlement with some uniformity in building size and layout. There is a strong association between the polygonal soil discoloration on the mound's surface, the mound's highpoints, and the distribution of Period I material. It would appear that this surface soil discoloration is attributable to more than just the Period I circumvallation.

The houses of the settlement were laid out in a ring around the High Mound (Figure 29). The intervening open areas were provided with a wall, and in some cases the houses abutted it. On the west side of Building I, this fortification wall appears to have been mudbrick. In other areas, the fortification wall was probably *tauf*, and structures of mudbrick, stone, and *tauf* abutted it. At angles and corners in the wall there were circular bastions probably 3 m in diameter (Building IV), whereas in other places square towers were used such as Building II, potentially Building V, and possibly to the southwest of Building III.

The entrance appears to have been where Stein placed it on his sketch map, just to the south of Operation L Building V (Figures 3 and 4; Stein 1940:379, Sketch Map 25). An alternative entrance might have been located at the south end of the settlement near Building I and the tower (Building II), perhaps even between these two structures in the earliest phase of construction. An entry here would accord well with the Mongol tendency to locate the main gate in the center of the southern wall (Masuya 1997:212).

There is also evidence of what may be a ditch outside the fortification wall west of Building III and at the north end of Operation VII J-K. The central part of the settlement was probably a large open space. In this area, the excavators found few stratified remains of Period I, except near the mound's central depression, where substantial stone footings and stone-paved steps were discovered.

The small finds from the site suggest that a typical range of domestic activities occurred in and around the houses, including food preparation, spinning, and weaving. Yet the ceramic assemblage, the size of Buildings I and III, and the fortification of the site belie a simple agricultural village and suggest a certain degree of affluence for some of the settlement's occupants and possibly a modest strategic significance for the location.

The closest parallels for the layout of the settlement are the hill forts at Taşkun Kale (ca. 1300-50 AD) in eastern Turkey and the earlier phases of Gritille (early 11th to mid 12th centuries) in southeastern Turkey (McNicoll 1983; Redford 1998). Like Hasanlu, both sites had a polygonal fortification wall with bastions and towers enclosing a roughly oval space (McNicoll 1983:7-12, fig. 4; Redford 1998:68-76; fig. 2.18). Buildings were built against and perpendicular to the interior face of the fortification wall. These structures were entered from a large open space at the center of the settlement.

The fortress or police post at Taşkun Kale, situated atop a *tepe* standing 7-8 m above the surrounding area, was the central focus of a larger Christian village covering at least 10 ha (McNicoll 1983:190). The fortress could house a garrison of 40-60 soldiers, who were probably responsible for policing the immediate region for the Ilkhanids. The garrison was probably not Christian.

The *kale* commanded the surrounding Murat valley and the important Aşvan/Harput road (McNicoll 1983:3). The fort is dated to the Ilkhanid period largely on the basis of the coins found at the site (McNicoll 1983:17-19). Its oval-shaped walls enclosed an area of approximately 40 x 30 m. At least five, and perhaps as many as eight, small rectangular towers (3.30 x 4.20 m) projected out from this wall at 10 m intervals. The curtain wall varied from .95 to 1.0 m wide, averaging 1.20 to 1.35 m. Spoke walls running perpendicular to the curtain wall divided the interior space into groups of garrison rooms, which were entered from a central open courtyard. The ceramics from the site are quite different from the Hasanlu I assemblage, with the exception of the ubiquitous green-glazed *sgraffiato* ware with abstract designs incised through a white slip (McNicoll 1983:60). Unlike Hasanlu, there was an absence of domestic debris from inside the *kale*.

The initial fortifications at Gritille (Phases 2 and 3) are linked to the Byzantine and Crusader periods (Redford 1998:270). Gritille lay in the hinterland of Samsat, and the hill fort probably served as one node in a defensive network in Samsat's hinterland. The fortification walls enclosed an area of at least 100 x 50 m. Like Taşkun Kale, the interior of the fort was divided by spoke walls that formed the boundaries for interior structures. The curtain wall, originally ca. 2.0 m wide, was reinforced with rectangular towers measuring 5.0 m wide and projecting 3.0 m out from the face of the wall.

As evidenced by Gritille, Taşkun Kale, and Hasanlu, there is a long history in the Medieval period in the Near East of locating small fortresses of similar design in advantageous positions in the countryside. Key considerations for their location appear to have been the lines of sight achieved from these high points for surveillance and their efficacy for controlling important roads, river crossings, water sources, and important agricultural and pastoral catchments in the hinterland of larger centers.

It is also possible, although less likely, that Hasanlu I functioned as a *ribāṭ*, a "small castellum or military guard post on the highway or frontier where cavalry attached (*rabaṭa*) their horses, but it developed a second meaning as post house, relay station, or caravanserai" (Blair 1986b:88, n.48). Some *ribāṭ*, served as rural caravanserais, providing lodging and furnished with servants (Blair 1986b:88-89, n.48). Hasanlu I would have been an extremely modest, rural version of a *ribāṭ*, when compared to the monumental example at Sarcham, dated by an inscription to 1332-33 AD (Wilber 1955:180, no. 90; fig. 57, pls. 188 and 189).

The ceramic assemblage, especially the lājvardīnah ware from Buildings I, III, and IV, securely dates the settlement to as early as the late 13 and early 14th centuries AD. The ubiquity of monochrome green-glazed ware akin to so-called Garrus Ware, while not particularly instructive for dating, does hint at a degree of continuity with Saljūq ceramic traditions, as does the incised and impressed buff ware assemblage. The absence of many of the attributes typical of standard Saljūq glazed earthenwares, such as certain styles of *sgraffiato* and champlevé decoration and most of the typical glaze colors, may provide a preliminary basis for distinguishing the Ilkhanid material from the Saljūq. This would prove especially useful to researchers undertaking archaeological surveys, where the likelihood of finding other unequivocal ceramic hallmarks of the Ilkhanid peri-

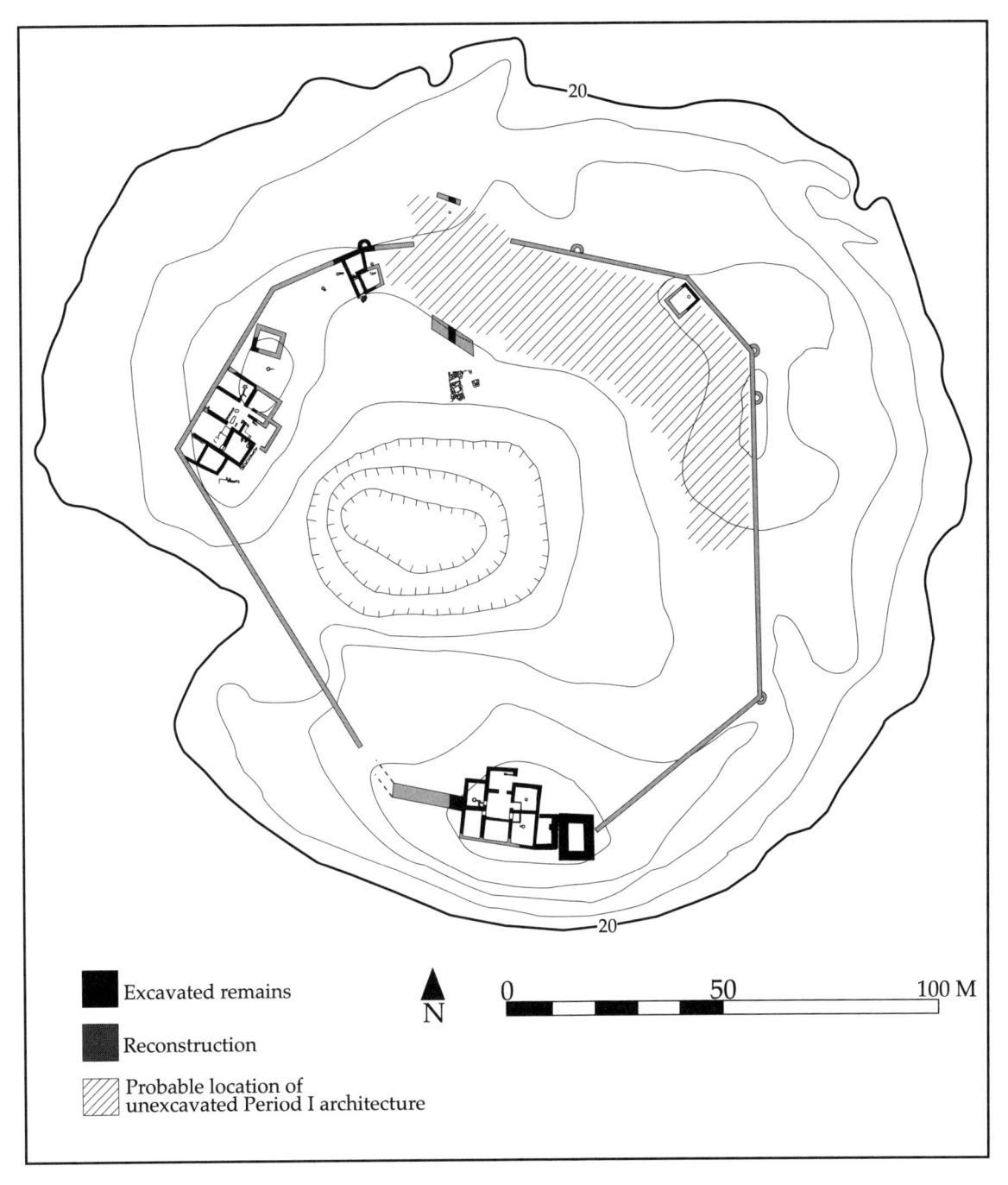

Figure 29. Hasanlu I: Site reconstruction based on aerial photos, Stein's 1936 sketch map, and the 1956-62 excavations.

od, such as lājvardīnah ware and a few types of underglaze decorated and luster wares, are probably relatively low on small-to-medium-sized sites due to the prestige-good status of these wares, not to mention the tendency of overglaze decoration to disintegrate when exposed to the elements. The resulting bias would be an overrepresentation of larger urban centers with access to fine glazed wares at the expense of villages and hamlets with a preponderance of locally produced unglazed wares and glazed earthenwares.

One other sobering possibility that might bias regional settlement data would be the attribution of small sites with monochrome glazed ware and unglazed earthenwares to the later Saljūq period and sites with a similar assemblage with the addition of lājvardīnah ware to the early Ilkhanid, when in fact socioeconomic differences, rather than chronological variation, was responsible for the pattern. In effect, affluent households with access to prestige ceramics from urban centers would be living in the Ilkhanid period (e.g., Hasanlu), while their poorer contemporaries were seemingly stranded in the Saljūq Period (e.g., Hajji Firuz Tepe and Dinkha Tepe). The planned layout and fortifications of Hasanlu imply the site was a node of central state control, perhaps a garrison and/or the abode of a local administrator, which might explain the higher status of the residents suggested by their access to urban prestige goods.

The absence of Saljūq fine glazed wares and those of the 15th century in Hasanlu I strengthens the Ilkhanid attribution. In the absence of more accurate means for dating—no coins were found in Hasanlu I deposits and radiocarbon samples were not collected from the upper strata—one cannot rule out extending the date of the occupation into the succeeding Chobanid (1335-43 AD) and early Jalayirid (1343-1432 AD) periods. However, arguments for the brief period of Hasanlu I construction at the site aside, there is no evidence for extending the date of the occupation into the period of Timūrīd influence and Qarā Qoyūnlū (1432-68 AD) and Āq Qoyūnlū (1468-1501 AD) suzerainty in Āzarbaijān (Woods 1999).

Ceramic groups typical of the late 14th and early 15th centuries are absent (see esp. Mason, Bailey, and Golombek 1996:111 ff.), such as glazed wares akin to Sīrāf Site E made of a petro-fabric linked to Diyarbākir and the Āq Qoyūnlū (Whitehouse 1969:56; Mason, Bailey, and Golombek 1996:115). Moreover, if several stylistic groups of blue and white and much of the material dubbed "Kubachi style" are in fact the product of Tabrīz during the Qarā Qoyūnlū and Āq Qoyūnlū periods (Golombek 1996:136-37; Lane 1939), which appears highly likely, one would certainly expect such ceramics to begin replacing the fine stone paste wares typical of Hasanlu I if occupation extended into the 15th century.

It is not surprising that the Ushnu-Sūldūz region would have been fairly extensively settled in the Ilkhanid period given the importance of northwestern Iran, and Āzarbaijān in particular, to the transhumant Mongols as summer pasture. The capitals of Tabrīz and Marāgheh, as well as lavish palaces such as those at ūjān and Takht-i Sulaimān (*Sughurluq*), were located in this general region (Figure 1). Moreover, a large number of the main Mongol summer and winter camps, *yaylaq* and *qïshlaq* respectively, were located not far to the east and south of Hasanlu. The important *qïshlaq* of Jaghatu was likely situated only 20-30 km to the east of Hasanlu in the vicinity of modern Sūldūz on the Zarīneh Rūd, also known as the Jaghatu Chāy. The propinquity of rural agricultural settlements to the seasonal encampments of the Mongols was linked to the feudal system whereby land and fiefs were granted as compensation for military service, or *iqṭā'*. As Petrushevsky points out, "Ḥamd Allāh Qazvīnī locates *iqṭā'* land in Āzarbaijān, Arrān, Shirvan, and Khurasan, which is completely explained by the fact that the main summer (*yailaq*) and winter (*qïshlaq*) camps of the Mongol and Turkish tribes forming the backbone of the Il-Khanid army were there. Cultivated land with settled peasants near to nomad camps was given as *iqṭā'*" (1968:518-19).

Hasanlu Tepe certainly lies in the purlieus of the Ilkhanid core area and appears to have been a prosperous, albeit short-lived, rural settlement, hill fortress, and/or *ribāṭ*. In the Ilkhanid period, favorable terms were offered to landowner tenants willing to resettle and improve abandoned lands (*khālisāt*) in an effort to boost the ruler's revenues

(Petrushevsky 1968:516-17). However, the expansion of the rural economy, begun with the establishment of Saljūq feudalism and furthered by Ghazan, probably did not last long. In the end, the overextension of the *iqṭāʿ* system under Ghazan and its metamorphosis under the Jalayirids into *soyurghal* vitiated rural production and probably contributed to the steady decline in settlement seen following the Ilkhanid period in the region and elsewhere (Petrushevsky 1968:518-20; Ashtor 1976:273). Moreover, depopulation comes as no surprise considering the historical milieu of the later 14th and 15th centuries. The Ilkhanid empire rapidly fragmented following the reign of Abū Saʿīd (1316-35). Nearly two centuries of political turmoil and destructive military campaigns followed, as the Chobanids, Jalayirids, the Golden Horde, Qarā Qoyūnlū, Āq Qoyūnlū, and Tīmūrids vied for control of the former Ilkhanid kingdom. During this chaos, Āzarbaijān was the main prize. Surely adding to the destabilization of rural settlement was the Black Death of 1347-50. The Hasanlu region was not resettled until the first half of the 19th century.

BIBLIOGRAPHY

Allan, J. W. 1971. *Mediaeval Islamic Pottery*. Oxford: Ashmolean Museum.

———. 1973. "Abū'l-Qāsim's Treatise on Ceramics." *Iran* 11:111-20.

———. 1974. "Incised Wares of Iran and Anatolia in the 11th and 12th Centuries." *Keramos* 64:15-22.

Allan, J. W., and Caroline Roberts, eds. 1990. *Three Studies in Medieval Ceramics*. Oxford: Oxford University Press.

Ashtor, E. 1976. *A Social and Economic History of the Near East in the Middle Ages*. Berkeley, CA: University of California Press.

Aslanov, G., B. Ibragimov, and S. Kaşkaj 1997. "Das mittelalterliche Haraba-Gilan (Azerbajdšan)." *Archäologische Mitteilungen aus Iran und Turan* 29:401-26.

Bivar, A. D. H. 2000. *Excavations at Ghubayrā, Iran*. London: School of Oriental and African Studies.

Bivar, A. D. H., and G. Féhérvári 1966. "The Walls of Tammisha." *Iran* 4:35-50.

Blair, Sheila S. 1986a. "The Mongol Capital of Sulṭāniyyeh, 'The Imperial'". *Iran* 25:139-51.
———. 1986b. *The Ilkhanid Shrine Complex at Natanz, Iran*. Harvard Middle East Papers, Classical Series 1. Cambridge, MA: Center for Middle Eastern Studies, Harvard University.

Boyle, J. A., ed. 1968. *The Cambridge History of Iran 5. The Saljuq and Mongol Periods*. Cambridge: The University Press.

Boyle, J. A. 1968. "Dynastic and Political History of the Īl-Khāns." *In* J. A. Boyle, ed., *The Cambridge History of Iran 5. The Saljuq and Mongol Periods*. Cambridge: The University Press, 303-421.

Broudy, Eric 1979. *The Book of Looms*. Hanover, NH: Brown University Press.

Browne, Edward G. 1951. *A Literary History of Persia 3*. Cambridge: The University Press.

Cassius Dio Cocceianus [1961]. *Dio's Roman History*. With an English translation by Earnest Cary, on the basis of the version of Herbert Baldwin Foster. Loeb Classical Library. Cambridge, MA: Harvard University Press.

Crane, Mary 1937. "II. The Historical Documents." *Bulletin of the American Institute for Iranian Art and Archaeology* 5/2:84-89.

Crowe, Yolande 1987. "Change in Style in Persian Ceramics in the Last Part of 7/13th C." *Rivista degli Studi Orientali* 59/1-4:47-55.

Danti, Michael D. Forthcoming. "The Medieval Remains from Hajji Firuz Tepe, Iran."

Dyson, Robert H., Jr. 1956. "Pennsylvania Survey in Iran." *Archaeology* 9 (4):284-5.

——— 1957. "Iran, 1956." *University Museum Bulletin* 21 (1):38.

——— 1958a. "Pennsylvania Campaign in Iran." *Archaeology* 11 (2):128.

——— 1958b. "Iran 1957: Iron Age Hasanlu." *University Museum Bulletin* 22 (2):25-32.

——— 1959. "Digging in Iran: Hasanlu, 1958." *Expedition* 1 (3):4-17.

——— 1960. "Hasanlu, Iran." *Expedition* 3 (1):11.

——— 1961. "Hasanlu, 1960 Campaign." *Archaeology* 14 (1):63-4.

——— 1983. "Introduction." *In* Mary M. Voigt, *Hajji Firuz Tepe, Iran: The Neolithic Settlement.* University Museum Monograph 50. Philadelphia: University of Pennsylvania Museum of Archaeology and Anthropology, xxv-xxviii.

——— 1999. "The Achaemenid Painted Pottery of Hasanlu IIIA." *Anatolian Studies* 49:101-10.

Eggebrecht, Arne, ed. 1989. *Die Mongolen und ihr Weltreich.* Mainz am Rhein: Philipp von Zabern.

Ettinghausen, Richard 1936. "New Affiliations for a Classical Persian Pottery Type." *Parnassus* 8:12.

——— 1939. "Ceramic Art in Islamic Times. B. Dated Faience." *In* A. U. Pope, ed., *A Survey of Persian Art* 2. London: Oxford University Press, 1667-96.

Féhérvári, Géza 2000. *Ceramics of the Islamic World in the Tareq Rajab Museum.* London: Tauris.

Ghirshman, R. 1939. *Fouilles de Sialk près de Kashan, 1933, 1934, 1937* 2. Paris: Librairie Orientaliste Paul Geuthner.

Gibson, McGuire, James A. Armstrong, and Augusta McMahon 1998. "The City Walls of Nippur and an Islamic Site Beyond: Oriental Institute Excavations, 17th Season, 1987." *Iraq* 60:11-44.

Golombek, Lisa 1996. "The Ceramic Industry in Fifteenth-century Iran: An Interpretation." *In* Lisa Golombek, Robert B. Mason, and Gauvin A. Bailey, eds., *Tamerlane's Tableware: A New Approach to the Chinoiserie Ceramics of Fifteenth- and Sixteenth-century Iran.* Costa Mesa, CA: Mazda, 124-39.

Golombek, Lisa, and Donald Wilber 1988. *The Timurid Architecture of Iran and Turan.* Princeton, NJ: Princeton University Press.

Golombek, Lisa, Robert B. Mason, and Gauvin A. Bailey, eds. 1996. *Tamerlane's Tableware: A New Approach to the Chinoiserie Ceramics of Fifteenth- and Sixteenth-century Iran.* Costa Mesa, CA: Mazda.

Grube, Ernst J. 1976. *Islamic Pottery of the Eighth to the Fifteenth Century in the Keir Collection.* London: Faber and Faber.

——— 1994. *Cobalt and Lustre: the First Centuries of Islamic Pottery.* Nasser D. Khalili Collection of Islamic Art 9. London: Nour Foundation.

Ḥākemī, 'Alī, and Maḥmūd Rād 1950. "Rapport et resultats de fouilles scientifiques à Hasanlu, Solduz." *Guzārishhā-yi bāstān-shināsī* 1:87-103.

Ḥamd Allāh Mustaufī Qazvīnī [1915-19]. *The Geographical Part of the Nuzhat-al-qulūb Composed by Hamd-Allāh Mustaufī of Qazwīn in 740 (1340)* 1. Vol. 2 edited and translated by Guy Le Strange. E. J. W. Gibb Memorial Series 23. Leiden: Brill.

Kiani, M. Y. 1978. *Iranian Pottery. A General Survey Based on the Prime Ministry of Iran's Collections.* Tehran: Prime Ministry of Iran.

Kleiss, W. 1982. "Qaleh Gabri, Naqarah Khaneh und Bordj-e Yazid bei Reyy." *Archaeologische Mitteilungen aus Iran* 15:311-28.

——— 1986. "Lang-i Rud, südöstlich von Qom. Festung, C(ch)ahar Taq und Siedlung." *Archaeologische Mitteilungen aus Iran* 19:191-210.

——— 1996. "Die Architektur des Mongolischen Gebäudes auf der sasanidischen Ufermauer." *In* W. Kleiss and P. Calmeyer, eds., *Bisitun. Ausgrabungen und Forschungen in den Jahren 1963-1967.* Teheraner Forschungen 7. Berlin: Gebr. Mann, 183-219.

——— 1997. "Bauten und Siedlungsplätze in der Umgebung von Soltaniyeh." *Archäologische Mitteilungen aus Iran und Turan* 29:341-44.

Komaroff, Linda 2002. "The Transmission and Dissemination of a New Visual Language." *In* Linda Komaroff and Stefano Carboni, eds. *The Legacy of Genghis Khan.* New York: Metropolitan Museum of Art, 168-96.

Komaroff, Linda, and Stefano Carboni, eds. 2002. *The Legacy of Genghis Khan.* New York: Metropolitan Museum of Art.

Lane, Arthur 1939. "The So-Called 'Kubachi' Wares of Persia." *Burlington Magazine* 75:156-62.

——— 1953, 1965. *Early Islamic Pottery: Mesopotamia, Egypt and Persia.* London: Faber and Faber.

——— 1957. *Later Islamic Pottery. Persia, Syria, Egypt, Turkey.* London: Faber and Faber.

Luschey-Schmeisser, Ingeborg 1990. "Eine Lüstre-Lagwardina-Kachel mit Krieger-Darstellung und einem Vers aus dem Helden-Epos." *Archäologische Mitteilungen aus Iran* 23:291-97.

——— 1996. "Die Keramik aus dem Mongolischen Gebäude." *In* W. Kleiss and P. Calmeyer, eds., *Bisitun. Ausgrabungen und Forschungen in den Jahren 1963-1967.* Teheraner Forschungen 7. Berlin: Gebr. Mann, pp. 221-40.

——— 2000. "Einige seldjuqische und mongolische baukeramische Fragmente aus Iran." *Archäologische Mitteilungen aus Iran und Turan* 32:361-409.

Mason, Robert B. 1997. "Mediaeval Iranian Lustre-Painted and Associated Wares: Typology in a Multidisciplinary Study." *Iran* 35:103-35.

Mason, Robert B., Gauvin A. Bailey, and Lisa Golombek 1996. "Stylistic Groups and Their Production Centres." *In* Lisa Golombek, Robert B. Mason, and Gauvin A. Bailey, eds., *Tamerlane's Tableware: A New Approach to the Chinoiserie Ceramics of Fifteenth- and Sixteenth-century Iran.* Costa Mesa, CA: Mazda, 109-23.

Masuya, Tomoko 1997. "The Ilkhanid Phase of Takht-i Suleimān." Ph.D. dissertation, Institute of Fine Arts, New York University.

——— 2002. "Ilkhanid Courtly Life." *In* Linda Komaroff and Stefano Carboni, eds., *The Legacy of Genghis Khan.* New York: Metropolitan Museum of Art, 74-103.

Melville, Charles 2002. "The Mongols in Iran." *In* Linda Komaroff and Stefano Carboni, eds., *The Legacy of Genghis Khan.* New York: Metropolitan Museum of Art, 36-61.

McNicoll, Anthony 1983. *Taşkun Kale. Keban Rescue Excavations Eastern Anatolia.* BAR International Series 168. Oxford: British Archaeological Reports.

Morgan, David 1990. *The Mongols*. Cambridge, MA: Blackwell.

Mostafavi, Mohamad Taghi 1960. "The Historical Remains of Hasanlu." *The Bulletin of Radio Iran, Aban Mah*. 1339 [1960] 51:12-13, 38.

Naumann, Elisabeth, and Rudolf Naumann 1969. "Ein Kösk im Sommerpalast des Abaqa Chan auf dem Takht-i Suleiman und seine Dekoration." *In* Oktay Aslanapa and Rudolf Naumannm, eds., *Forschungen zur Kunst Asiens. In Memoriam Kurt Erdmann*. Istanbul Üniversitesi Edebiyat Fakültesi. Türk ve Islām Sanati Kürsüsü. Istanbul: Baha Matbaasi, 35-65.

Naumann, Rudolf 1963. "Eine keramische Werkstatt des 13. Jahrhundert auf dem Takht-i Suleiman." *In* Oktay Aslanapa, ed., *Beiträge zur Kunstgeschichte Asiens. In Memoriam Ernst Diez*. Istanbul Üniversitesi Edebiyat Fakültesi. Sanat Tarihi Enstitüsü 1. Istanbul: Baha Matbaasi, 301-7.

1971. "Brennöffen für Glasurtechnik." *Istanbuler Mitteilungen* 21:173.

1974. "Vorbericht über die Ausgrabungen auf dem Taxt-e Soleymān 1973." *In* Firouz Bagherzadeh, ed., *Proceedings of the IInd Annual Symposium on Archaeological Research in Iran*. Tehran: Iranian Centre for Archaeological Research, 194-215.

1977. *Die Ruinen von Tacht-e Suleiman und Zendan-e Suleiman*. Berlin: Dietrich Reimer.

Naumann, Rudolf, and Elisabeth Naumann 1976. *Takht-i Suleiman. Ausgrabung des Deutschen Archäologischen Instituts in Iran*. Ausstellungskataloge der Prähistorischen Staatssammlung 3. Munich: Prähistorische Staatssammlung.

Petrushevsky, I. P. 1968. "The Socio-Economic Condition of Iran under the Īl-Khāns." *In* J. A. Boyle, ed., *The Cambridge History of Iran 5. The Saljuq and Mongol Periods*. Cambridge: The University Press, 483-537.

Pinder-Wilson, R. H. 1969. *Islamic Pottery, 800-1400 AD*. An Exhibition arranged by the Islamic Art Circle and held at the Victoria and Albert Museum 1 October to 30 November 1969. Uxbridge, Middlesex: Westminster Press.

Phillips, E. D. 1969. *The Mongols*. London: Thames and Hudson.

Pope, Arthur Upham, ed. 1938-39. *A Survey of Persian Art from Prehistoric Times to the Present*. London: Oxford University Press.

Porada, Edith 1959. "The Hasanlu Bowl." *Expedition* 1(3):19-22.

1967. "Notes on the Gold Bowl and Silver Beaker from Hasanlu." *In* Arthur Upham Pope, ed., *A Survey of Persian Art from Prehistoric Times to the Present* 14. London: Oxford University Press, 2971-78.

Redford, Scott 1998. *The Archaeology of the Frontier in the Medieval Near East: Excavations at Gritille, Turkey*. Archaeological Institute of America Monographs, n. s. 3. Philadelphia, PA: University Museum/AIA.

Rossabi, Morris 2002. "The Mongols and Their Legacy." *In* Linda Komaroff and Stefano Carboni, eds., *The Legacy of Genghis Khan*. New York: Metropolitan Museum of Art, 12-35.

Rougeulle, Axelle 2001. "Harbâ, un site medieval tardif de l'Iraq central." *In* Catherine Breniquet and Christine Kepinski, eds., *Études Mésopotamiennes*. Bibliothèque de la Délégation Archéologique Française en Iraq 10. Paris: Éditions Recherche sur les Civilisations, 389-405.

Safar, Fuad 1945. *Wasit: The Sixth Season's Excavations*. Cairo: Imprimerie de l'Institute Français d'Archéologie Orientale.

Schmidt, Erich F. 1940. *Flights over Ancient Cities of Iran*. Chicago, IL: University of Chicago Press.

Schnyder, R. 1972. "Saljuq Pottery in Iran." *In The Memorial Volume of the Vth International Congress of Iranian Art & Archaeology* 2. Teheran: Ministry of Culture and Arts, 189-97.

——— 1974. "Mediaeval Incised Wares from Northwest Iran." *In* M. Watson, ed., *The Art of Iran and Anatolia from the 11th to the 13th century A.D.* Colloquies on Art & Archaeology in Asia. London: University of London, Percival David Foundation of Chinese Art, 85-94.

Soustiel, J. 1985. *La Céramique islamique: le guide du connaisseur*. Fribourg, Switzerland: Office du Livre.

Voigt, Mary M. 1976. "Hajji Firuz Tepe: An Economic Reconstruction of a Sixth Millennium Community in Western Iran." Ph.D. dissertation, Department of Anthropology, University of Pennsylvania.

——— 1983. *Hajji Firuz Tepe, Iran: The Neolithic Settlement*. Hasanlu Excavation Reports 1. University Museum Monograph 50. Philadelphia, PA: University of Pennsylvania Museum of Archaeology and Anthropology.

Watson, Oliver 1985. *Persian Lustre Ware*. London: Faber and Faber.

Watson, O., and V. Porter 1979. "Persian Silhouette-Ware and the Development of Underglaze Painting." *In* Margaret Medley, ed., *Decorative Techniques and Styles in Asian Ceramics*. Colloquies on Art and Archaeology in Asia 8. London: Percival David Foundation of Chinese Art, 86-103.

Weiers, Michael 1989. "Geschichte der Mongolen." *In* Arne Eggebrecht, ed., *Die Mongolen und ihr Weltreich*. Mainz am Rhein: Philipp von Zabern, 45-225.

Whitehouse, D. 1969. "Excavations at Siraf: Second Interim Report." *Iran* 7:39-62.

Wilber, Donald N. 1938. "The Parthian Structures at Takht-i-Sulayman." *Antiquity* 12(4):389-410.

——— 1955. *The Architecture of Islamic Iran: The Il-Khānid Period*. Princeton Oriental Studies 17. Princeton, NJ: Princeton University Press.

Wilkinson, Charles K. 1973. *Nishapur: Pottery of the Early Islamic Period*. New York: Metropolitan Museum of Art.

Willey, Peter 1963. *The Castles of the Assassins*. London: George G. Harrap.

Woods, John E. 1999. *The Aqquyunlu. Clan, Confederation, Empire*. Salt Lake City, UT: The University of Utah Press.

Wulff, Hans E. [1966]. *The Traditional Crafts of Persia*. Cambridge, MA: MIT Press.

Plates

Plate A. Aerial view of Hasanlu Tepe and the villages of Hasanlu and Aminlu taken in 1937 by Erich Schmidt (northwest at top). The excavated areas on the north edge of High Mound were dug by Sir Aurel Stein in 1936.

Plate B. Aerial view of Hasanlu Tepe and the village of Hasanlu taken from the southeast in 1957 by Harold Josef, the American Consul in Tabrīz. The line of the Ilkhanid fortification wall, the innermost circumvallation, is clearly visible, as is the WWI military trench on the edge of the upper High Mound. The trenches on the High Mound (Operations I, II, and VII) were dug by the Hasanlu Expedition in 1956 and 1957.

Plate C. Aerial view of Hasanlu Tepe in 1962 taken by Vaughn Crawford from the south looking north.

Plate D. Operation XXXIX (Grid BB28) Building I Rooms 1 and 4 during excavation in 1959 from the east looking west. The doorway from Room 1 to Room 4 and the oven in Room 4 are in the foreground. In the background are the remains of Burned Building IW of Period IVB and associated ancillary structures.

Plate E. Operation XXXIX (Grid BB28) from the west during excavation in 1959 showing the oven in Building I Room 4 in the foreground. Note the bin in the southeast corner.

Plate F. Operation XXXIX (Grid BB28) from the southwest showing Building I Room 4, the oven, and a bin.

Plate G. Operation XXXIV (CC30) taken in 1960 from the northeast, showing the stone footings of Building II Phase 1.

Plate H. Plaster with wood lathe impressions from Building III Room 2 (HAS 62-9).

Plate J. Grid U23 Building III Room 3, looking northeast during excavation and showing features abutting the northeast wall.

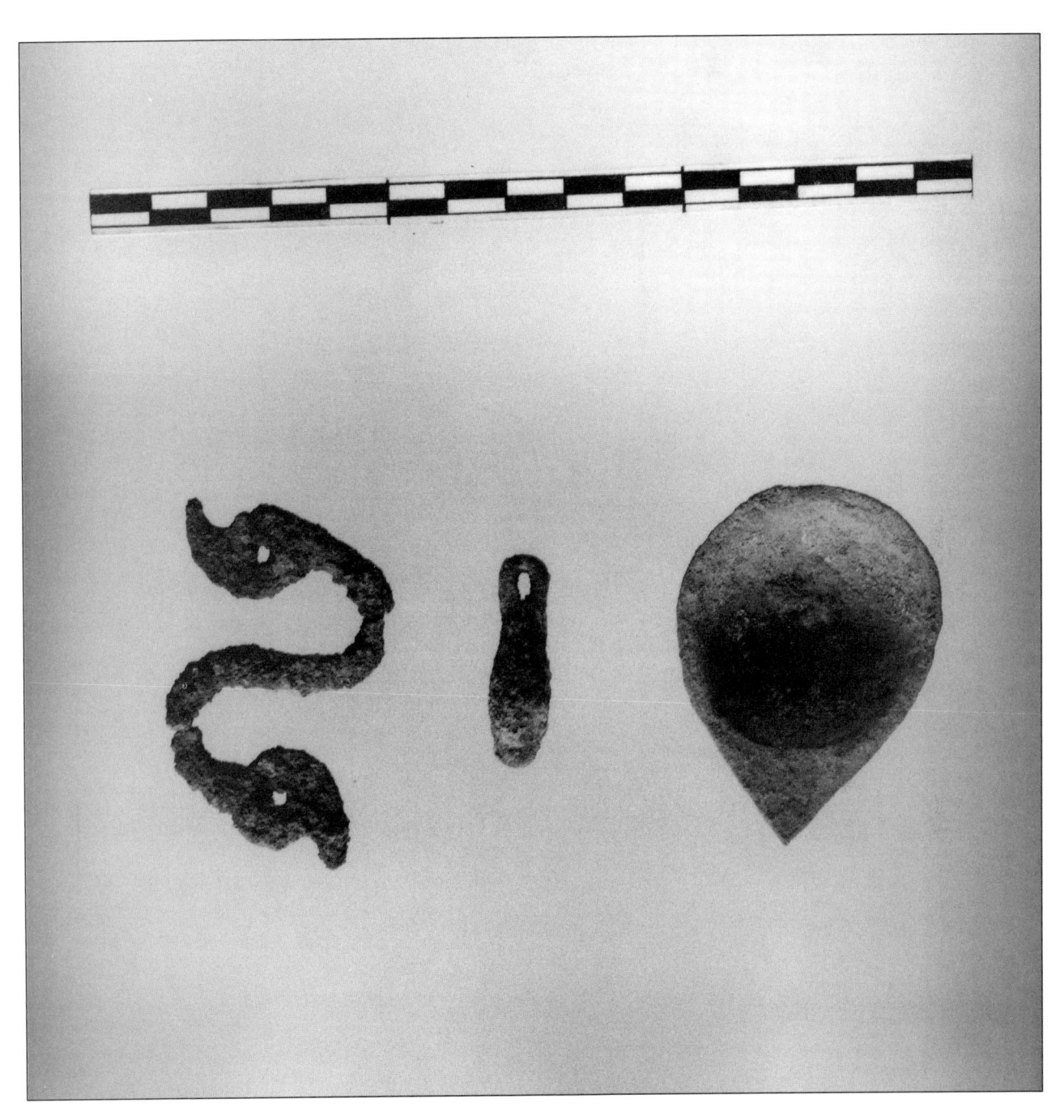

Plate K. Objects from Building III (l. to r.) HAS 62-17, HAS 62-1, and HAS 62-22.

Plate L. Grid U23 Building III Room 4 looking east showing the washbasin or toilet, the clay pipe drain, and the clay-lined drainage pit.

Plate M. Grid U23 Building III Room 4 looking west showing the washbasin or toilet, the clay pipe drain, and the clay-lined drainage pit.

Plate N. Grid T23 Building III Room 6 looking north, showing the oven, flue, and screen wall.

Plate O. Grid T23 Building III Room 6 looking southwest, showing the oven, flue, and screen wall.

Plate P. Lājvardīnah ware jar sherds (HAS 62-10, MET 63.109.25) from Building III Room 8.

Plate Q. Objects from Operation L and other contexts. Back row (l. to r.) HAS 59-338, HAS 59-330, HAS 59-336a, HAS 59-336b; Row 3, UPM 60-20-302, HAS 59-340 (not from Op. L); Row 2, unidentified glass fragment, HAS 59-333b; Row 1, HAS 59-333a.

Plate R. Buff ware lantern from Operation L (HAS 59-331).

Index

Abaqa 59
Abū'l-Qāsim 22-23
Abū Sa'īd 67
Aghkand Ware 61
aivān structures 59
'Alā' al-Dīn Muḥammad Shāh I 23
Āmul Ware 61
Aq Qoyūnlū 66-67
Arrān 66
Āzarbaijān 26, 66-67

Baghdad 2
Black Death 67
buff ware 22-23, 33, 36, 49, 59
Building I 9-11, 14
Building II 10-11, 14, 22
Building III 9-10, 27
Building IV 10, 31, 36
Building V 9, 49

Caspian Sea 61
ceramics, recovery methods 22
champlevé 61, 64
Chobanid Period 66-67
cooking pot ware 49

Dinkha Tepe 62, 66
Diyarbākir 66
Dyson, Robert H., Jr. 1, 7, 59

earthenwares 22
Ettinghausen Collection 23
excavation procedures 8

Farhādī 7
Field Number 8
fortification, Period I i, 2, 9, 27, 31, 33, 43, 45, 63, 64

Gadār River xiii, 1, 62
Garrus Ware 36, 59, 61-62, 64
Ghabri Ware, see Garrus Ware
Ghazan 67
Ghubayrā 63
glazed wares 22
Grid Designation 8
Gritille 64

Hajji Firuz Tepe 62, 66
Ḥākemī, 'Alī 7
Ḥamd Allāh Qazvīnī 66
Haraba-Gilan 36
Harbâ 63
Hasanlu II 11
Hasanlu IIIB 8-9
Hasanlu IVB 8
Hasanlu Number 8
Hasanlu sequence 2
hill forts 64

iqṭā' 66-67
Ismā'īlīs 61

Jaghatu 2, 66
Jaghatu Chāy 66
Jalayirid Period 66-67
Jis 59
Joseph, Harold xiii

Kel-i Shin Pass 2
khāliṣāt 66
Khurasan 66
Kubachi style 66

lājvardīnah ware 22, 23, 31, 33, 36, 42, 61-62, 64, 66

Lake Urmīyeh xiii, 1-2
luster-painted ware 22, 36, 62

Marāgheh 66
Media Atropatene 59
mīnā'i ware 22
Mongol conquests 61
monochrome green-glazed ware 22, 25, 30, 33, 36, 61, 64
mudbrick 11, 27, 31

Naqadeh xiii
Naumann, Rudolph 59
Nippur 63
Nishapur 23
Northern Stratigraphic Trench 43-45

Object Number 8
Öljeitü 59
Operation Number 8
ovens 11, 14, 30-31, 43, 59
overglaze painted ware 22, 25, 33, 36, 42, 62

pastoralism 66
Perso-Russian War 1
Praaspa 59

Qarā Qoyūnlū 66-67
qïshlaq 66

Rād, Maḥmūd 7
Rashīd al-Dīn 23
red ware 22-23, 30, 33, 36, 49, 59
ribāṭ 64, 66
Rowanduz Pass 2
rural development 61, 66-67

Saljūq Period 22, 23, 59, 61-62, 64, 66-67
Samarqand 23
Samsat 64
Sarcham 64
Schmidt, Erich F. xiii, 7
sgraffiato 22, 36, 59, 61, 64
Shāhnāma 62
Shirvan 66
Shīz 59
Sīrāf 66
soyurghal 67
splash glazing 61
Stein, Sir Aurel xiii, 6, 62
Stratum Number 8
Sughūrlūq/Saturiq 59, 66
Sūldūz 1, 66
Sulṭānābād ware 33, 42, 62
Sulṭānīyeh 23, 59

Tabrīz 23, 61, 66
Takht-i Sulaimān 23, 36, 42, 59, 61-63
Taşkun Kale 63-64, 93
tauf 14, 27, 31, 33, 63
tile, ceramic 62-63

ūjan 66
underglaze painted ware 22, 36, 62
Ushnu 1, 62

Wasiṭ 63
weaving implements 49

yaylaq 66

Zagros Mountains 1-2
Zarīneh Rūd 66